THE DEATH PENALTY and the disadvantaged

IDEAS in CONFLICT

Gary E. McCuen

GEM
GARY McCUEN
publications inc.

411 Mallalieu Drive
Hudson, Wisconsin 54016
Phone (715) 386-7113

Illustration and Photo Credits

Carol ★ Simpson 11, 21, 157; U.S. Department of Justice 33; Steve Kelley 79; Dick Locher 91; Craig MacIntosh 25, 125; Eleanor Mill 85; Steve Sack 47, 150; Bill Sanders 105; Wayne Stayskal 133; Richard Wright 41.

© 1997 by Gary E. McCuen Publications, Inc.
411 Mallalieu Drive, Hudson, Wisconsin 54016

(715) 386-7113

International Standard Book Number
0-86596-140-9
Printed in the United States of America

CONTENTS

Ideas in Conflict

Chapter 4   **THE DEATH PENALTY AND THE**
               DISADVANTAGED

REASONING SKILL DEVELOPMENT

These activities may be used as individualized study guides for students in libraries and resource centers or as discussion catalysts in small group and classroom discussions.

IDEAS
in CONFLICT

This series features ideas in conflict on political, social, and moral issues. It presents counterpoints, debates, opinions, commentary, and analysis for use in libraries and classrooms. Each title in the series uses one or more of the following basic elements:

Introductions that present an issue overview giving historic background and/or a description of the controversy.

Counterpoints and debates carefully chosen from publications, books, and position papers on the political right and left to help librarians and teachers respond to requests that treatment of public issues be fair and balanced.

Symposiums and forums that go beyond debates that can polarize and oversimplify. These present commentary from across the political spectrum that reflect how complex issues attract many shades of opinion.

A *global* emphasis with foreign perspectives and surveys on various moral questions and political issues that will help readers to place subject matter in a less culture-bound and ethnocentric frame of reference. In an ever-shrinking and interdependent world, understanding and cooperation are essential. Many issues are global in nature and can be effectively dealt with only by common efforts and international understanding.

Reasoning skill study guides and discussion activities provide ready-made tools for helping with critical reading and evaluation of content. The guides and activities deal with one or more of the following:

RECOGNIZING AUTHOR'S POINT OF VIEW

INTERPRETING EDITORIAL CARTOONS

VALUES IN CONFLICT

WHAT IS EDITORIAL BIAS?

WHAT IS SEX BIAS?

WHAT IS POLITICAL BIAS?

WHAT IS ETHNOCENTRIC BIAS?

WHAT IS RACE BIAS?

WHAT IS RELIGIOUS BIAS?

From across **the political spectrum** *varied sources are presented for research projects and classroom discussions. Diverse opinions in the series come from magazines, newspapers, syndicated columnists, books, political speeches, foreign nations, and position papers by corporations and nonprofit institutions.*

About the Editor

Gary E. McCuen is an editor and publisher of anthologies for libraries and discussion materials for schools and colleges. His publications have specialized in social, moral and political conflict. They include books, pamphlets, cassettes, tabloids, filmstrips and simulation games, most of them created from his many years of experience in teaching and educational publishing.

CHAPTER 1

THE DEATH PENALTY: METHOD AND HISTORY

SENTENCED TO WHAT KIND OF DEATH?

AN OVERVIEW OF EXECUTION METHODS

Dr. Jack Kevorkian

Jack Kevorkian, M.D., has gained international media attention within the past decade for his work in assisting terminally ill patients to end their lives.

■ POINTS TO CONSIDER

1. Identify the various methods of execution employed before the 19th century.

2. Give a brief chronology of execution methods in the modern era. What sentiment or ideology has driven the evolution of execution methods, according to Kevorkian.

3. Indicate how methods of execution have evolved in the United States over the past two centuries.

Excerpted from Dr. Jack Kevorkian, M.D. **Prescription: Medicide.** Prometheus Books, Amherst, NY: 1991. Reprinted by permission.

The Chinese also resorted to the so-called thousand cuts whereby an executioner would slowly and deliberately cut into and cut off parts of the body so skillfully that death occurred only after the thousandth cut.

EXECUTION METHODS IN HISTORY

Methods of execution have somehow always fulfilled the aims of torture and revenge – nowadays surreptitiously – and usually in a highly dramatic way. The ancient Hebrews and Assyrians buried the condemned alive. Crucifixion was also popular, until abolished by Constantine in A.D. 325. It was usually performed by breaking the condemned's leg bones, seating him on a bar fastened to the post of a wooden cross, and pinning his now very flexible legs beneath him with a nail through the feet. The outstretched arms were attached to the crossbar with nails through the hands, and the victim was allowed to suffer there until dead.

During mass executions in the Roman Coliseum many simultaneously crucified criminals were smeared with tar and set ablaze at night to form spectacular human torches. The ancient Greeks used the wheel, later resurrected in sixteenth-century France and Germany. With this method a heavy bar or hammer was used to break almost every bone in the limbs, hips, and shoulders of a victim who had been laid on a horizontal wheel. The flailed limbs were braided around the rim. Death resulted either from blows to the chest and head, or from prolonged exposure aloft on the elevated wheel.

Men, and especially women, in pre-Christian Britain and Rome were executed by drowning in ponds and marshes. During these early times beheading by sword was also common and generally reserved for highly respected or aristocratic individuals. This tradition continued into nineteenth-century Europe.

In eighth-century England the Danes executed criminals by throwing them off cliffs. A century or so later the Britons resorted to the ancient practice of stoning people to death. In thirteenth-century England the gibbet appeared and became so popular that gallows were to be seen almost everywhere.

The gibbet was the forerunner of modern hanging. The victim was placed in chains, or in a specially constructed body cage of

Cartoon by Carol ★ Simpson. Reprinted by permission.

latticed iron, and hoisted onto a wooden crossbar. He hung there until dead or until some compassionate countryman killed him to end his suffering. It wasn't until the eighteenth century that the "drop" (the counterpart of our modern trapdoor) was introduced. The assumption was (and apparently still is) that breaking the condemned's neck was a more "humane" way to kill. This method is still in use today in the United States.

Criminals were burned alive in wicker baskets as sacrifices to gods in pre-Christian Europe. At the same time burning alive at the stake was common in Britain, a method used for the wholesale slaughter of many thousands of heretics and apostates during the Middle Ages. The agony of victims was frequently eased by compassionate executioners who would subtly tighten the restraining cord around the neck for a tolerable death by strangulation before flames reached the flesh.

Other novel and gruesome methods were devised by the end of the sixteenth century. In Russia some criminals were dragged to death tied to the tails of horses, while others were strapped to the backs of wild beasts and sent off to die in the forests. In England they were sometimes pressed to death under increasingly heavy weights. Occasionally the victim's friends would add their own body weight to the load to cut short the suffering. In Spain execution often was by garroting, through the tightening of a steel collar against a backboard until the neck was broken. Whipping to death with intertwined thongs and metal wires was common in medieval Britain and Russia. Boiling to death was used for a short while in England under Henry VIII. And in India the criminal lay on the ground or knelt over a tree stump to have his head squashed under an elephant's foot.

A couple of particularly repugnant methods were used in China. One consisted of placing live criminals in crude coffins and sawing them in half lengthwise from head to crotch. This unspeakably brutal method was used in Spain as late as the nineteenth century, where the victim was sawn while positioned upside down to intensify and prolong the suffering. The Chinese also resorted to the so-called thousand cuts whereby an executioner would slowly and deliberately cut into and cut off parts of the body so skillfully that death occurred only after the thousandth cut. This extraordinary ritual made allowances for gradations of condemnation: executioners with less rancor called for the curtailed suffering of only ten or one hundred cuts.

Constant complaints from executioners in medieval England about difficulty in keeping their swords sharp and keeping many restive criminals in place during decapitation led to the development of "beheading machines." The earliest examples appeared in thirteenth-century Europe...

Without much doubt the most gruesome method in the Western world was drawing and quartering. In the Middle Ages the procedure consisted of having horses drag (or draw) a criminal to a public square. Drawing alone caused so much physical trauma and even occasional death that, in time, a type of sledge was used to carry the criminal behind the horse. At the square the criminal was hanged on a gibbet, later taken down alive, disemboweled, and then decapitated. The headless body was then cut into quarters and all parts were stuffed into a basket for public display...

THE RISE OF "HUMANITARIAN" EXECUTION

This was happening at a time when serious debate was begin-

CAPITAL PUNISHMENT AND THE U.S. COURTS

The American colonies, inheriting English law and criminal practice, provided for capital punishment for several crimes, though the number and type of capital offenses varied from one jurisdiction to another. However, several 18th and 19th century reformers criticized the use of the death penalty as unreasonable and inhumane. For example, the American Society for the Abolition of Capital Punishment was organized in 1845, and in 1847, Michigan, still a territory, abolished capital punishment for all crimes, except treason. Other states, though less so in the South, reduced the number of offenses for which the death penalty was required, usually limiting them to murder, treason, and a few other offenses.

Though the death penalty continued to be imposed during the 20th century, with over 3,800 civilian prisoners executed between 1930 and 1972, the number of executions decreased from a high of 199 in 1935 to a low of only one in 1966. In *Furman v. Georgia* (1972), the U.S. Supreme Court held unconstitutional the imposition of the death penalty under state law permitting juries unfettered discretion in capital sentencing, but upheld the imposition of such penalties four years later in sentencing systems that provided guidelines for the exercise of jury or court discretion.

Most states have enacted new death penalty laws since 1972, adhering to constitutional requirements. At present, the U.S. Government and 38 states permit the imposition of the death penalty. Methods of execution include lethal injection, electrocution, the gas chamber, hanging, and the firing squad.

Since the 1976 reinstatement of capital punishment, a total of 263 executions have been carried out. The annual number of executions remained below three until 1982, rose precipitously in the mid-1980s to a high of 25 in 1987, and again in the early-1990s to a high of 38 in 1993. As of January 31, 1995, one report enumerates 2,976 inmates awaiting execution.

"Capital Punishment," Congressional Research Service Report for Congress, April 17, 1995.

ning to rage over the morality of judicial killing and over the relative merits of how it was done. Humanitarian demands for less torturous methods seemed to be on the verge of satisfaction when thoughts turned in the late nineteenth century to the increasing knowledge and practical application of electricity. At the same time, legislators and penal authorities in the State of New York resolved that shooting and hanging were too gruesome; they opted instead for the "clean" method of electrocution. Their specially built mahogany chair was used for the first time to execute a murderer in August, 1890.

The novelty quickly spread to other states, despite official reports of unintentional agonizing results from prolonged electrocution due to equipment failure, misjudgment of body resistance, and bickering among officials about who was to throw the switch...

Bad experiences with electrocution in the opening decade of the present century prompted authorities in Nevada to turn to the use of hydrogen cyanide as the death-dealing agent, and in 1924 the gas chamber made its debut.

Lethal injection rounds out the brief history of execution methods into the late twentieth century. This technique causes a serene, rapid death from the intravenous injection of three drugs in mixed solution: a fast-acting barbiturate for almost instantaneous unconsciousness, a muscle paralyzer to stop breathing and to avert convulsions, and potassium chloride to stop the heart. It was adopted as the official method by the Oklahoma legislature in 1977, but was first used in Texas in 1982.

From this review one might conclude that methods of execution have become progressively more humane during the present century. However, a valid assessment demands critical analysis of the mechanism involved for each method.

ELECTROCUTION IN THE MODERN ERA

Electricity causes biological damage through both heat and electrochemical havoc. Heat denatures (or inactivates) protein by coagulating it, thereby doing away with its biological function through the destruction of enzymes, hormones, and even tissue structure. The electrical current itself nullifies the function of organs and tissues such as the brain, nerves, and heart by overwhelming the fragile bioelectrical basis of their metabolism. The

14

voltage applied is not the critical factor but is, in fact, almost irrelevant as mere electrical "pressure." The body can tolerate millions of volts without discomfort...

The type of electrical current, too, makes a difference – whether direct (DC) or alternating (AC). The latter is more dangerous and can be lethal even with low voltage and relatively low amperage. The alternating cycle of 60 per second, which is ordinary 110-120 volt house current, can be extremely dangerous and, without producing excessive heating, will invariably stop heart action through standstill or ventricular fibrillation if the body somehow becomes part of the circuit. That often happens accidentally in the home when someone's body is immersed in or in good contact with water, which turns the body into an electrical conductor...

THE GAS CHAMBER

When sodium cyanide pellets are dropped into acid beneath the seated subject in a gas chamber, extremely lethal hydrogen cyanide (chemical symbol HCN) is produced...Cyanide asphyxiates by choking the cells instead of blocking air intake. The gas, HCN, is rapidly absorbed into the bloodstream through the lungs – much faster than a solution of cyanide is absorbed through the stomach. The red blood cells are relatively immune to HCN. But when delivered to all other body cells...cyanide literally and rapidly chokes all the body's cells to death at the same time. It doesn't take much HCN to induce death: concentrations of as little as 200-300 parts of cyanide per million parts of air can do it...

THE EXECUTION CONTROVERSY

The subject of intensive debate and research in nineteenth-century Europe was whether consciousness persists for any time at all after decollation. The question was important because the number of executions by sword and guillotine was large and increasing during a simultaneous wave of humanitarian concern sweeping the continent...

From observation of muscular reactions to mechanical and electrical stimuli applied to various parts of the head, including the cut ends of muscles and spinal cord in the neck, one group of investigators concluded that perception of pain persists for a short interval, perhaps as long as fifteen minutes after beheading...

But another research team disagreed emphatically. This latter group postulated that consciousness was due to some sort of ethereal life essence that they called "nerve fluid." The flow of that hypothetical "fluid" through nerves toward the brain supposedly produced awareness; and away from the brain, as would be the case with massive drainage of the "fluid" from the nervous tissue transected by the decapitation, would have to result in instantaneous unconsciousness. The controversy became very heated and so popular that it was made a regular feature in daily newspapers...

HANGING PROPONENTS

The question of how hanging affects consciousness soon complicated matters. Proponents of hanging as a more humane method objected to the practice of beheading...Advocates of hanging argued that if the noose were correctly applied to the neck, consciousness would disappear quickly due to the sudden and complete damming of blood in the head, with resultant swelling of the brain and rupture of small blood vessels. As proof they cited the testimony of individuals who had been rescued from the gallows: these people swore that there was no pain before they lost consciousness...

In a sense any advantages of hanging would seem to have been compromised when the "drop" was added. That embellishment usually results in the breaking of the neck and the ripping of the spinal cord, thus essentially and much more crudely duplicating the results of decapitation without detaching the head... Proponents of hanging were then embarrassed at having to face the criticism they originally leveled at beheading...

THE BIRTH OF ELECTROCUTION

Thomas Edison was to revolutionize civilization yet again by saying that while he opposed capital punishment, electricity would do the job. Edison had motives of his own. It was the dawning of the electric age. Electricity was perceived as a frightening and dangerous thing, and Edison exploited that fear by trying to use it against his rival George Westinghouse. Westinghouse had developed the alternating current system which we now use, while Edison favored direct current and wanted to persuade the public that the Westinghouse system was more dangerous than his own. What better way than to say his rival system could effectively kill a man...

Twenty-five people were there to witness the world's first electrocution [Aug. 6, 1890], and as writer Richard Moran describes it, the first 17-second jolt seemed to work. The condemned, William Kembler, slumped over in his chair...

But then all of a sudden, he came to life, or he appeared to come to life, and somebody in the crowd yelled, "Kembler lives, he's alive, turn back the juice," and that's what happened. They then turned the juice back on for four minutes. It was finally turned off when Kembler's body caught fire, began to smolder and burn. Indeed, Kembler was so burned that the doctors could not examine him, pronounce him dead, for about 15 minutes, his body was just too hot...

One headline the next day read, "Kembler-Westinghouse." Westinghouse himself said the execution was so botched they could have done better with an axe.

"History of Capital Punishment in New York," National Public Radio's **All Things Considered**, broadcast January 23, 1995.

LETHAL INJECTION

What about lethal injection? Surely that recent innovation constitutes definite progress...Thiopental sodium is a fast-acting barbiturate that produces almost instantaneous short-term unconsciousness after a single dose. It is also used as a "truth serum" administered in small, intermittent, carefully calibrated hypnotic doses while the subject counts backward from 100. A trance-like semi-consciousness is usually reached before the count gets to 90.

Succinylcholine is a muscle paralyzer...By paralyzing the muscles of the body, succinylcholine counteracts the tendency of thiopental to cause muscle tremors or more violent contractions. That assures a surgeon that the patient's body will remain calm and at complete rest, and an executioner that the condemned's body will not react.

To complete the lethal mixture for execution, society has stipulated the addition of potassium chloride. A high level of potassium in the blood paralyzes the heart muscle. In effect, then, that would correspond to a heart attack for the condemned while in the deep sleep of barbiturate coma (which certainly cannot be said to be cruel or barbaric).

As was the case with electrocution, lethal injection soon spread to other states in short order and is now fast becoming predominant. As of April, 1991, the method of execution in twenty-one states is lethal injection. Six states grant a choice: between lethal injection and the gas chamber in Missouri and North Carolina, hanging in Montana and Washington, or a firing squad in Idaho and Utah. There is little doubt that from an objective standpoint it is the method of choice at present, especially as far as those who observe executions are concerned. But, according to some critics, that may not be true for the condemned.

Like its predecessors, lethal injection as now practiced may be melodrama with the inherent risk of overkill. Critics argue that the combination of drugs raises the possibility of a sometimes prolonged and unintentionally agonizing death. For example, if the doses of thiopental and potassium chloride are not big enough to cause immediate death, the condemned could slowly suffocate because of the succinylcholine's paralysis of muscles used for breathing; and the total paralysis of all muscles would make it impossible for even a conscious subject to make that known. According to a few witnesses, that rare possibility may have already happened during recent executions...

The first such execution in Texas in 1982 was attempted by prison employees. They had great difficulty in trying to pierce the badly scarred veins of the condemned man with a large needle, and blood was spattered all over the sheets. Among those witnessing the bungled attempt was the prison doctor...

THE GOAL OF PUNISHMENT

Science really can't help us much in deciding on the one best method. In general it tends to be a selection based on common sense and an indefinable "gut" feeling. Now admittedly this is a precarious way to deal with a profound dilemma. There is a much better way, but it will take effort.

Thus far we have been discussing only the "what" and the "how" of capital punishment. The "what" is self-explanatory. But if we are to identify the best of the "how," the best way to carry it out, then we'll have to answer the hardest question of all – the "why" of capital punishment. And that will take more than plain common sense and a "gut" feeling. That awesome obligation calls for the invocation of a uniquely human and frequently abused faculty – ratiocination, exact thinking applied to what society says the aim of the death penalty should be and what the aim really is.

INTERPRETING EDITORIAL CARTOONS

This activity may be used as an individualized study guide for students in libraries and resource centers or as a discussion catalyst in small group and classroom discussions.

Although cartoons are usually humorous, the main intent of most political cartoonists is not to entertain. Cartoons express serious social comment about important issues. Using graphic and visual arts, the cartoonist expresses opinions and attitudes. By employing an entertaining and often light-hearted visual format, cartoonists may have as much or more impact on national and world issues as editorial and syndicated columnists.

Points to Consider:

1. Examine the cartoon on the next page.

2. How would you describe the message of the cartoon? Try to describe the message in one to three sentences.

3. Do you agree with the message expressed in the cartoon? Why or why not?

4. Does the cartoon support the author's point of view in any of the readings in this publication? If the answer is yes, be specific about which reading or readings and why.

5. Is the reading in Chapter One in basic agreement with the cartoon?

"IT'S A STAY OF EXECUTION. CNN WANTS A BETTER CAMERA ANGLE."

Cartoon by Carol ★ Simpson. Reprinted by permission.

CHAPTER 2

THE DEATH PENALTY AND RACE

McCLESKEY v. KEMP: THE POINT

Justice Lewis Powell, Jr.

Former Supreme Court Justice Lewis Powell, Jr. wrote the majority opinion in McCleskey v. Kemp (1987). In the majority opinion, joined by Chief Justice Rehnquist, Justices White, O'Connor, and Scalia, Justice Powell held that the statistical evidence of the petitioner, Warren McCleskey, was insufficient to prove his discrimination claims under the Eighth and Fourteenth Amendments of the Constitution.

■ POINTS TO CONSIDER

1. According to the opinion of the court, what must McCleskey prove in order to claim discrimination under the Fourteenth Amendment?

2. Evaluate the reasons the majority on the Court found that the Baldus study failed to prove discrimination.

3. Discuss the importance of "discretion" by the jury, judge and all other players in the criminal justice system.

4. Summarize the fear of Justice Powell concerning the use of statistical evidence in discrimination claims that challenge the constitutionality of sentencing. How might factors other than race play a role?

Excerpted from the majority opinion of the United States Supreme Court in **McCleskey v. Kemp** (1987) 481 US 279, 95 L Ed 2d 262, 107S Ct 1756.

At most, the Baldus study indicates a discrepancy that appears to correlate with race. Apparent disparities in sentencing are an inevitable part of our criminal justice system.

McCleskey, a black man, was convicted of two counts of armed robbery and one count of murder in the Superior Court of Fulton County, Georgia, on October 12, 1978. McCleskey's convictions arose out of the robbery of a furniture store and the killing of a white police officer during the course of the robbery.

The jury convicted McCleskey of murder. At the penalty hearing, the jury heard arguments as to the appropriate sentence. Under Georgia law, the jury could not consider imposing the death penalty unless it found beyond a reasonable doubt that the murder was accompanied by one of the statutory aggravating circumstances. The jury in this case found two aggravating circumstances to exist beyond a reasonable doubt: the murder was committed during the course of an armed robbery, and the murder was committed upon a peace officer engaged in the performance of his duties. In making its decision whether to impose the death sentence, the jury considered the mitigating and aggravating circumstances of McCleskey's conduct. McCleskey offered no mitigating evidence. The jury recommended that he be sentenced to death on the murder charge and to consecutive life sentences on the armed robbery charges. The court followed the jury's recommendation and sentenced McCleskey to death.

BALDUS STUDY

(Professor David Baldus of the University of Iowa examined records of the U.S. District Court of the Northern District of Georgia. In death penalty cases, he claimed to find statistical proof for discrimination by race.)

At most, the Baldus study indicates a statistical discrepancy that appears to correlate with race. Apparent disparities in sentencing are an inevitable part of our criminal justice system. The discrepancy indicated by the Baldus study is "a far cry from any major systemic defects." Our consistent rule has been that constitutional guarantees are met when "the mode [for determining guilt or punishment] itself has been surrounded with safeguards to make it as fair as possible," Singer v. United States. In light of the safeguards designed to minimize racial bias in the process, the fundamental value of jury trial in our criminal justice system, and the benefits

Reprinted with permission from the **Star Tribune**, Minneapolis. Illustration by Craig MacIntosh.

that discretion provides to criminal defendants, we hold that the Baldus study does not demonstrate a constitutionally significant risk of racial bias affecting the Georgia capital sentencing process.

14TH AMENDMENT AND EQUAL PROTECTION

McCleskey's first claim is that the Georgia capital punishment statute violates the Equal Protection Clause of the Fourteenth Amendment. He argues that race has infected the administration of Georgia's statute in two ways: persons who murder whites are more likely to be sentenced to death than persons who murder blacks, and black murderers are more likely to be sentenced to death than white murderers.

As a black defendant who killed a white victim, McCleskey claims that the Baldus study demonstrates that he was discriminated against because of his race and because of the race of his victim. Our analysis begins with the basic principle that a defendant who alleges an equal protection violation has the burden of proving "the existence of purposeful discrimination." Whitus v. Georgia. Thus, to prevail under the Equal Protection Clause, McCleskey must prove that the decision-makers in his case acted with discriminatory purpose. He offers no evidence specific to his own case that would support an inference that racial considerations played a part in his sentence. Instead, he relies solely on the Baldus study. McCleskey argues that the Baldus study compels an inference that his sentence rests on purposeful discrimination. McCleskey's claim that these statistics are sufficient proof of discrimination, without regard to the facts of a particular case, would extend to all capital cases in Georgia, at least where the victim was white and the defendant is black.

McCleskey's statistical proffer must be viewed in the context of his challenge. McCleskey challenges decisions at the heart of the State's criminal justice system. Implementation of laws necessarily requires discretionary judgments. Because discretion is essential to the criminal justice process, we would demand exceptionally clear proof before we would infer that the discretion has been abused. The unique nature of the decisions at issue in this case also counsels against adopting such an inference from the disparities indicated by the Baldus study. Accordingly, we hold that the Baldus study is clearly insufficient to support an inference that any of the decision-makers in McCleskey's case acted with discriminatory purpose.

WITHOUT INTENT TO DISCRIMINATE

McCleskey also suggests that the Baldus study proves that the State as a whole has acted with a discriminatory purpose. He appears to argue that the State has violated the Equal Protection Clause by adopting the capital punishment statute and allowing it to remain in force despite its allegedly discriminatory application. For this claim to prevail, McCleskey would have to prove that the Georgia Legislature enacted or maintained the death penalty statute because of an anticipated racially discriminatory effect. In Gregg v. Georgia, this Court found that the Georgia capital sentencing system could operate in a fair and neutral manner. There was no evidence then, and there is none now, that the Georgia Legislature enacted the capital punishment statute to further a racially discriminatory purpose.

Nor has McCleskey demonstrated that the legislature maintains the capital punishment statute because of the racially disproportionate impact suggested by the Baldus study. As legislatures necessarily have wide discretion in the choice of criminal laws and penalties, and as there were legitimate reasons for the Georgia Legislature to adopt and maintain capital punishment, (see Gregg v. Georgia), we will not infer a discriminatory purpose on the part of the State of Georgia. Accordingly, we reject McCleskey's equal protection claims.

CRUEL AND UNUSUAL PUNISHMENT

McCleskey also argues that the Baldus study demonstrates that the Georgia capital sentencing system violates the Eighth Amendment. The Eighth Amendment prohibits infliction of "cruel and unusual punishments." Chief Justice Warren, writing for the plurality in Trop v. Dulles, acknowledged the constitutionality of capital punishment. In his view, the "basic concept underlying the Eighth Amendment" in this area is that the penalty must accord with "the dignity of man." In applying this mandate, we have been guided by his statement that "the Amendment must draw its meaning from the evolving standards of decency that mark the progress of a maturing society."

Two principal decisions guide our resolution of McCleskey's Eighth Amendment claim. In Furman v. Georgia, the Court concluded that the death penalty was so irrationally imposed that any particular death sentence could be presumed excessive.

In Gregg v. Georgia (1976) the Court specifically addressed the question left open in Furman – whether the punishment of death for murder is "under all circumstances, 'cruel and unusual' in violation of the Eighth and Fourteenth Amendments of the Constitution." "The most marked indication of society's endorsement of the death penalty for murder [was] the legislative response to Furman." During the four-year period between Furman and Gregg, at least 35 states had reenacted the death penalty.

Numerous features of the then new Georgia statute met the concerns articulated in Furman. Our decisions since Furman have identified a constitutionally permissible range of discretion in imposing the death penalty. First, there is a required threshold below which the death penalty cannot be imposed. In this context, the State must establish rational criteria that narrow the decision-maker's judgment as to whether the circumstances of a particular defendant's case meet the threshold. Moreover, a societal consensus that the death penalty is disproportionate to a particular offense prevents a State from imposing the death penalty for that offense.

McCleskey cannot argue successfully that his sentence is "disproportionate to the crime in the traditional sense." See Pulley v. Harris. He does not deny that he committed a murder in the course of a planned robbery, a crime for which this Court has determined that the death penalty constitutionally may be imposed. McCleskey argues that the sentence in his case is disproportionate to the sentences in other murder cases.

Because McCleskey's sentence was imposed under Georgia sentencing procedures that focus discretion "on the particularized nature of the crime and the particularized characteristics of the individual defendant," we lawfully may presume that McCleskey's death sentence was not "wantonly and freakishly" imposed, and thus that the sentence is not disproportionate within any recognized meaning under the Eighth Amendment.

McCleskey contends that the Georgia capital punishment system is arbitrary and capricious in application, and therefore his sentence is excessive, because racial considerations may influence capital sentencing decisions in Georgia.

To evaluate McCleskey's challenge, we must examine exactly what the Baldus study may show. Even Professor Baldus does not contend that his statistics prove that race enters into any capital sentencing decisions or that race was a factor in McCleskey's particular case. Statistics at most may show only a likelihood that a particular factor entered into some decisions. There is, of course, some risk of racial prejudice influencing a jury's decision in a criminal case. There are similar risks that other kinds of prejudice will influence other criminal trials. The question "is at what point that risk becomes constitutionally unacceptable," Turner v. Murray. McCleskey asks us to accept the likelihood allegedly shown by the Baldus study as the constitutional measure of an unacceptable risk of racial prejudice influencing capital sentencing decisions. This we decline to do.

JURY DISCRETION

Because of the risk that the factor of race may enter the criminal justice process, we have engaged in "unceasing efforts" to eradicate racial prejudice from our criminal justice system. (Batson v. Kentucky) Our efforts have been guided by our recognition that "the inestimable privilege of trial by jury...is a vital principle, underlying the whole administration of criminal justice," ex parte Milligan.

The capital sentencing decision requires the individual jurors to focus their collective judgment on the unique characteristics of a particular criminal defendant. It is not surprising that such collective judgments often are difficult to explain. But the inherent lack of predictability of jury decisions does not justify their condemnation. On the contrary, it is the jury's function to make the difficult and uniquely human judgments that defy codification and that "build discretion, equity, and flexibility into a legal system." H. Kalven and H. Zeisel, *The American Jury* 498 (1966).

McCleskey's argument that the Constitution condemns the discretion allowed decision-makers in the Georgia capital sentencing system is antithetical to the fundamental role of discretion in our criminal justice system. Discretion in the criminal justice system offers substantial benefits to the criminal defendant. Not only can a jury decline to impose the death sentence; it can decline to convict or choose to convict of a lesser offense. Whereas decisions against a defendant's interest may be reversed by the trial judge or on appeal, these discretionary exercises of leniency are final and unreviewable.

BOUNDLESS CHALLENGES

If we accepted McCleskey's claim that racial bias has impermissibly tainted the capital sentencing decision, we could soon be faced with similar claims as to other types of penalty. Moreover, the claim that his sentence rests on the irrelevant factor of race easily could be extended to apply to claims based on unexplained discrepancies that correlate with membership in other minority groups, and even to gender.

CONCLUSION

As we have stated specifically in the context of capital punishment, the Constitution does not "place totally unrealistic conditions on its use," Gregg v. Georgia. McCleskey's arguments are best presented to the legislative bodies. It is not the responsibility – or indeed even the right – of this Court to determine the appropriate punishment for particular crimes. It is the legislatures, the elected representatives of the people, that are "constituted to respond to the will and consequently the moral values of the people," Furman v. Georgia. Legislatures also are better qualified to weigh and "evaluate the results of statistical studies in terms of their own local conditions and with a flexibility of approach that is not available to the courts," Gregg v. Georgia. Capital punishment is now the law in more than two-thirds of our states. It is the ultimate duty of courts to determine on a case-by-case basis whether these laws are applied consistently with the Constitution. Despite McCleskey's wide-ranging arguments that basically challenge the validity of capital punishment in our multiracial society, the only question before us is whether in his case, the law of Georgia was properly applied. We agree with the District Court and the Court of Appeals for the Eleventh Circuit that this was carefully and correctly done in this case.

READING

3

McCLESKEY v. KEMP: THE COUNTERPOINT

Justice William Brennan

Justice William Brennan authored one of the dissents in the 1987 Supreme Court decision, McCleskey v. Kemp. Justice Marshall joined him in his dissent; Justices Blackmun and Stevens joined in part.

■ POINTS TO CONSIDER

1. What significance does Justice Brennan place upon the factor of race and history in his dissent?

2. Contrast the ideas of risk of discrimination and proof of discrimination. How has the court in the past treated the risk of discrimination, according to Brennan. How should the Baldus evidence be treated?

3. For Justice Brennan, why is rationality and scrutiny in capital sentencing procedures, as opposed to other punishments, so important? How have Brennan and past Justices displayed special scrutiny in capital sentencing procedures?

Excerpted from the dissenting opinion of Justice William Brennan in the United States Supreme Court decision, **McCleskey v. Kemp** (1987) 481 US 279, 95 L Ed 2d 262, 107 S Ct 1756.

Decisions influenced by race rest in part on a categorical assessment of the worth of human beings according to color, insensitive to whatever qualities the individuals in question may possess.

At some point in this case, Warren McCleskey doubtless asked his lawyer whether a jury was likely to sentence him to die. A candid reply to this question would have been disturbing. Counsel would feel bound to tell McCleskey that defendants charged with killing white victims in Georgia are 4.3 times as likely to be sentenced to death as defendants charged with killing blacks.

The Court today holds that Warren McCleskey's sentence was constitutionally imposed. It finds no fault in a system in which lawyers must tell their clients that race casts a large shadow on the capital sentencing process. The Court arrives at this conclusion by stating that the Baldus study cannot "prove that race enters into any capital sentencing decisions or that race was a factor in McCleskey's particular case." Since, according to Professor Baldus, we cannot say "to a moral certainty" that race influenced a decision, we can identify only "a likelihood that a particular factor entered into some decisions," and "a discrepancy that appears to correlate with race." This "likelihood" and "discrepancy," holds the Court, is insufficient to establish a constitutional violation.

BURDEN OF PROOF

The Court assumes the statistical validity of the Baldus study, and acknowledges that McCleskey has demonstrated a risk that racial prejudice plays a role in capital sentencing in Georgia. Nonetheless, it finds the probability of prejudice insufficient to create constitutional concern.

Close analysis of the Baldus study, however, in light of both statistical principles and human experience, reveals that the risk that race influenced McCleskey's sentence is intolerable by any imaginable standard. The Baldus study indicates that, after taking into account some 230 nonracial factors that might legitimately influence a sentencer, the jury more likely than not would have spared McCleskey's life had his victim been black.

32

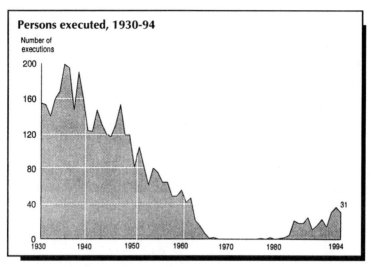

Persons executed, 1930-94

Number of
executions

Source: Bureau of Justice Statistics

HISTORY OF BIAS

Evaluations of McCleskey's evidence cannot rest solely on the numbers themselves. We must also ask whether the conclusion suggested by those numbers is consonant with our understanding of history and human experience. Georgia's legacy of a race-conscious criminal justice system, as well as this court's own recognition of the persistent danger that racial attitudes may affect criminal proceedings, indicates that McCleskey's claim is not a fanciful product of mere statistical artifice.

For many years, Georgia operated openly and formally precisely the type of dual system the evidence shows is still effectively in place. The criminal law expressly differentiated between crimes committed by and against blacks and whites, distinctions whose lineage traced back to the time of slavery. During the colonial period, black slaves who killed whites in Georgia, regardless of whether in self-defense or in defense of another, were automatically executed. A. Higginbotham, *In the Matter of Color: Race in the American Legal Process* 256 (1978).

This Court has invalidated portions of the Georgia capital sentencing system three times over the past 15 years. The specter of race discrimination was acknowledged by the Court in striking down the Georgia death penalty statute in Furman.

Historical review of Georgia criminal law is not intended as a bill of indictment calling the State to account for past transgressions. Citation of past practices does not justify the automatic condemnation of current ones. But it would be unrealistic to ignore the influence of history in assessing the plausible implications of McCleskey's evidence.

No guidelines govern prosecutorial decisions to seek the death penalty, and Georgia provides juries with no list of aggravating and mitigating factors, nor any standard for balancing them against one another. Once a jury identifies one aggravating factor, it has complete discretion in choosing life or death, and need not articulate its basis for selecting life imprisonment. The Georgia sentencing system therefore provides considerable opportunity for racial considerations, however subtle and unconscious, to influence charging and sentencing decisions.

History and its continuing legacy thus buttress the probative force of McCleskey's statistics. Formal dual criminal laws may no longer be in effect, and intentional discrimination may no longer be prominent. Nonetheless, as we acknowledged in Turner, "subtle, less consciously held racial attitudes" continue to be of concern, and the Georgia system gives such attitudes considerable room to operate. The conclusions drawn from McCleskey's statistical evidence are therefore consistent with the lessons of social experience.

The majority thus misreads our Eighth Amendment jurisprudence in concluding that McCleskey has not demonstrated a degree of risk sufficient to raise constitutional concern. It must first and foremost be informed by awareness of the fact that death is irrevocable, and that as a result "the qualitative difference of death from all other punishments requires a greater degree of scrutiny of the capital sentencing determination," California v. Ramos.

RACE AND DISCRETION OF THE JURY

Decisions influenced by race rest in part on a categorical assessment of the worth of human beings according to color, insensitive to whatever qualities the individuals in question may possess. Enhanced willingness to impose the death sentence on black defendants, or diminished willingness to render such a sentence when blacks are victims, reflects a devaluation of the lives of black persons. When confronted with evidence that race more likely than not plays such a role in a capital-sentencing system, it is plainly insufficient to say that the importance of discretion demands that the risk be higher before we will act – for in such a case the very end that discretion is designed to serve is being undermined.

On the basis of the need for individualized decisions, it rejects evidence, drawn from the most sophisticated capital sentencing analysis ever performed, that reveals that race more likely than not infects capital sentencing decisions.

CHALLENGING GEORGIA'S SAFEGUARDS

Gregg bestowed no permanent approval on the Georgia system. It simply held that the State's statutory safeguards were assumed sufficient to channel discretion without evidence otherwise. It has now been over 13 years since Georgia adopted the provisions upheld in Gregg. Professor Baldus and his colleagues...produced striking evidence that the odds of being sentenced to death are significantly greater than average if a defendant is black or his or her victim is white. The challenge to the Georgia system is not speculative or theoretical; it is empirical. As a result, the Court cannot rely on the statutory safeguards in discounting McCleskey's evidence, for it is the very effectiveness of those safeguards that such evidence calls into question.

TOO MUCH JUSTICE?

The Court next states that its unwillingness to regard the petitioner's evidence as sufficient is based in part on the fear that recognition of McCleskey's claim would open the door to widespread challenges to all aspects of criminal sentencing. Taken on its face, such a statement seems to suggest a fear of too much justice. Yet surely the majority would acknowledge that if striking evidence indicated that other minority groups, or women, or even persons with blond hair, were disproportionately sentenced to death, such a state of affairs would be repugnant to deeply rooted conceptions of fairness. The prospect that there may be more widespread abuse than McCleskey documents may be dismaying, but it does not justify complete abdication of our judicial role.

To reject McCleskey's powerful evidence on this basis is to ignore both the qualitatively different character of the death penalty and the particular repugnance of racial discrimination, considerations which may properly be taken into account in determining whether various punishments are "cruel and unusual." Furthermore, it fails to take account of the unprecedented refinement and strength of the Baldus study.

It hardly needs reiteration that this Court has consistently acknowledged the uniqueness of the punishment of death. "Death, in its finality, differs more from life imprisonment than a 100-year prison term differs from one of only a year or two. Because of that qualitative difference, there is a corresponding difference in the need for reliability in the determination that death is the appropriate punishment," Woodson v. NC. Even those who believe that society can impose the death penalty in a manner sufficiently rational to justify its continuation must acknowledge that the level of rationality that is considered satisfactory must be uniquely high. As a result, the degree of arbitrariness that may be adequate to render the death penalty "cruel and unusual" punishment may not be adequate to invalidate lesser penalties. What these relative degrees of arbitrariness might be in other cases need not concern us here; the point is that the majority's fear of wholesale invalidation of criminal sentences is unfounded.

Despite its acceptance of the validity of Warren McCleskey's evidence, the Court is willing to let his death sentence stand because it fears that we cannot successfully define a different standard for lesser punishments. This fear is baseless. Finally, the

Court justifies its rejection of McCleskey's claim by cautioning against usurpation of the legislatures' role in devising and monitoring criminal punishment.

Those whom we would banish from society or from the human community itself often speak in too faint a voice to be heard above society's demand for punishment. It is the particular role of courts to hear these voices, for the Constitution declares that the majoritarian chorus may not alone dictate the conditions of social life. The Court thus fulfills, rather than disrupts, the scheme of separation of powers by closely scrutinizing the imposition of the death penalty.

PAST, PRESENT, FUTURE

It has been scarcely a generation since this Court's first decision striking down racial segregation, and barely two decades since the legislative prohibition of racial discrimination in major domains of national life. These have been honorable steps, but we cannot pretend that in three decades we have completely escaped the grip of a historical legacy spanning centuries. Warren McCleskey's evidence confronts us with the subtle and persistent influence of the past. His message is a disturbing one to a society that has formally repudiated racism, and a frustrating one to a Nation accustomed to regarding its destiny as the product of its own will. Nonetheless, we ignore McCleskey at our peril, for we remain imprisoned by the past as long as we deny its influence in the present.

The Court's decision today will not change what attorneys in Georgia tell other Warren McCleskeys about their chances of execution. Nothing will soften the harsh message they must convey, nor alter the prospect that race undoubtedly will continue to be a topic of discussion. McCleskey's evidence will not have obtained judicial acceptance, but that will not affect what is said on death row. However many criticisms of today's decision may be rendered, these painful conversations will serve as the most eloquent dissents of all.

READING

4

THE RACIAL JUSTICE ACT

House Judiciary Committee

The following statement was taken from a House Judiciary report on the Racial Justice Act. The report explained the purpose of the Racial Justice Act which was debated in the Congress and defeated.

■ **POINTS TO CONSIDER**

1. Why are legislative bodies rather than the courts responding to the issue of racial justice and the death penalty?

2. According to the reading, what does the Racial Justice Act entail?

3. Discuss the role of statistical analysis in determination of race bias.

4. What is the main source of disparity in capital sentencing? What are some suggestions to remedy this?

Excerpted from the House Judiciary Committee Report on the Racial Justice Act, March 24, 1994.

Clearly, few people today would admit an intent to discriminate. Therefore, the Supreme Court has usually recognized that the existence of illegal discrimination can be established by showing that the results of a decision-making process are discriminatory.

In 1987, the Supreme Court ruled in McCleskey v. Kemp, 481 U.S. 279, that courts could not accept evidence of discriminatory death sentencing patterns to prove the purposeful racial discrimination necessary to make out a claim under the Fourteenth Amendment. The Court held that someone challenging a death sentence had to prove that the prosecutor, judge or jury in his particular case consciously intended to discriminate on the basis of race. It held that the results of the decisions by prosecutors, judges and juries over the course of many cases could not prove such intentional discrimination.

At the close of the majority opinion in McCleskey, Justice Powell stated that arguments about the persistent pattern of racially discriminatory death sentencing were "best presented to the legislative bodies," which could develop appropriate responses.

RACIAL JUSTICE ACT

The Racial Justice Act responds to the McCleskey Court's invitation through the exercise of Congress's enforcement power under Section 5 of the Fourteenth Amendment. The Act would make it unlawful to carry out a sentence of death imposed on the basis of the race of the defendant or victim, and it would allow persons under sentence of death to challenge their sentences (but not their convictions) by using evidence that shows a pattern of racially discriminatory death sentencing, comparing similar cases and taking into account the brutality of the offenses, the prior records of the offenders or other statutorily appropriate non-racial characteristics.

The Act is a civil rights measure and adopts evidentiary procedures similar to those employed against racial discrimination in other civil rights laws. It is based on the realization that prosecutors, judges and jurors will rarely if ever admit that they were purposefully discriminatory in seeking or imposing the death penalty in a particular case. The Act allows the use of statistical evidence to establish an inference of racial discrimination.

The Act imposes a substantial burden on a person seeking to invoke its protections. First, the death penalty defendant must compile and analyze the data showing a pattern of racial disparity in the jurisdiction where he was sentenced and at the time he was sentenced. He must show that the disparity is significant. He must show that his case fits the pattern of racially discriminatory sentencing.

At any point in the process, the Government can stop the challenge by showing that the defendant's statistics are invalid as being incomplete or failing to account for relevant factors. Or the Government can show that the defendant's case does not fit the pattern of discriminatory sentences, by showing, for example, that the facts of the case fall into a category of highly aggravated cases where death is imposed regardless of race.

This orderly mechanism for proving racial discrimination in death sentencing is the same mechanism that Congress has adopted in other civil rights laws. It is the same approach that the Supreme Court itself has used in judging other claims of racial discrimination in the criminal justice system.

The Act will not abolish the death penalty. Nor will it force prosecutors to "relitigate every death penalty case," as some opponents have claimed. States will be free to carry out all their death sentences unless a significant racially discriminatory pattern can be shown. States will have an opportunity to challenge the adequacy of the statistical case itself – including the sufficiency of the data and the quality and results of the statistical analysis used to support it – as well as an opportunity to rebut any inference of racial bias by showing that any apparently racial pattern is explained by non-racial factors. Even if a state cannot explain a particular racial pattern, it can continue to carry out any sentences that do not fit within the pattern, i.e., sentences imposed in cases which reveal no racially-biased pattern of sentencing. The Act prohibits only the execution of those death sentences that are the product of racial bias.

The Act will not lead to death sentencing quotas. Rather, the purpose of the Act is to eliminate race from the decision whether to seek the death penalty. It encourages prosecutors (a) to develop non-racial standards for deciding when to seek death and (b) to apply those standards uniformly and consistently. A state cannot comply with the Act by adopting racial quotas; in fact, such quotas would violate the Act. If a prosecutor sought the death sen-

40

Cartoon by Richard Wright. Reprinted by permission.

tence on the basis of race, rather than on the basis of the circumstances of the crimes and the backgrounds of the defendants, the evidentiary principles established by the Act would reveal the discriminatory pattern, since the Act defines impermissible racial discrimination as a pattern of sentencing disparities that exists after accounting for non-racial factors.

USE OF STATISTICS IN PROVING RACE DISCRIMINATION

Statistical analyses are generally accepted as reliably measuring the influence of racial discrimination in complex decision-making processes. The Racial Justice Act is consistent with other civil rights laws under which an inference of racial discrimination can be established through the use of statistical evidence showing a significant racially discriminatory effect.

Clearly, few people today would admit an intent to discriminate. Therefore, the Supreme Court has usually recognized that the existence of illegal discrimination can be established by showing that the results of a decision-making process are discriminatory.

In the criminal justice area, for example, the Supreme Court has held that a black criminal defendant can establish a *prima facie* case of discrimination in the jury composition process by showing a substantial statistical disparity between the percentage of blacks in the population and the percentage of blacks in the pool from which his grand jury or trial jury was selected. Castaneda v. Partida , 430 U.S. 482 (1977). The Supreme Court has also granted relief when the result of the prosecutor's decisions to strike jurors peremptorily was the disproportionate elimination of black jurors and the prosecutor could not provide adequate non-racial reasons for the peremptory strikes. Batson v. Kentucky, 476 U.S. 79 (1986).

Where the Court has rejected evidence of discriminatory impact, Congress has exercised its enforcement authority by statutorily prohibiting unexplained and unjustified racial disparities. For example, when the Supreme Court ruled in City of Mobile v. Bolden, 446 U.S. 55 (1980), that the Voting Rights Act and the Fifteenth Amendment required a showing of discriminatory intent, Congress amended the Act to allow plaintiffs to base a showing of discrimination on evidence of discriminatory impact.

The Congress has the power under the Fourteenth Amendment to take remedial measures that eliminate not only overt race discrimination but also practices that entail a significant risk that persons of different races are being treated differently. The exercise of Congress' "safeguarding" role is especially appropriate where the death penalty is involved, for there "is a qualitative difference between death and any other permissible form of punishment," and hence, "a corresponding difference in the need for reliability in the determination that death is the appropriate punishment in a specific case." Zant v. Stephens, 462 U.S. 862, 884-85 (1983).

HOW STATES CAN RESPOND TO THE ACT

States will not be barred from using the death penalty because they can ensure that their capital sentencing practices do not lead to any significant pattern of racial discrimination.

The main source of disparity appears to be prosecutorial decisions, the area where meaningful change can be achieved most readily. Under guided discretion statutes, prosecutors still have wide discretion in deciding when to seek the death penalty. Thus, for example, states could provide clearer guidance to prosecutors, through statutory change or other directive. As Justice Stevens pointed out in his dissent in McCleskey,

> One of the lessons of the Baldus study is that there exist certain categories of extremely serious crimes for which prosecutors consistently seek, and juries consistently impose, the death penalty without regard to the race of the victim or the race of the offender. If Georgia were to narrow the class of death-eligible defendants to those categories, the danger of arbitrary and discriminatory imposition of the death sentence would be significantly decreased if not eradicated. — 481 U.S. at 367.

Another mechanism that could provide protection against racial discrimination is the proportionality review that most state supreme courts are required to conduct in each capital case in order to determine whether the sentence is proportionate to the penalties imposed in other cases. Many supreme courts only look to other cases in which the death sentence was imposed. The proportionality review would be much more likely to identify and correct racial bias if the reviewing court considered not only cases in which death was imposed but also death-eligible cases in which a life sentence was imposed.

READING

5

THE EFFECTIVE ABOLISHMENT OF THE DEATH PENALTY

Henry J. Hyde

Henry Hyde is a Republican congressman from Illinois. He wrote the following dissent from the House Judiciary Report on the Racial Justice Act.

■ POINTS TO CONSIDER

1. What does the author fear the Racial Justice Act will essentially do?

2. How does the author use "mitigating" and "aggravating" circumstances to explain why many studies show that murderers who kill white victims are more likely to receive a death sentence?

3. Discuss why Henry Hyde feels that the Racial Justice Act "offends the notion of individualized justice."

4. Contrast the Racial Justice Act with alternative legislation such as the Equal Justice Act mentioned in the reading.

Excerpts of dissenting views from a report on the Racial Justice Act by the House Judiciary Committee, March 24, 1994.

In the Racial Justice Act, death penalty opponents are simply attempting to do indirectly what they have been unable to do directly – abolish the death penalty.

The objection to this proposal is the same as it was when this legislation was considered in 1990 and 1991. We are opposed to the "Racial Justice Act" because its likely effect will be the invalidation of every capital sentence now in effect as well as prevention of the use of capital punishment in the United States. This is not because racial prejudice permeates the criminal justice system, but because the proposal would impose unrealistic burdens of proof on the prosecution in response to alleged statistical disparities.

MISLEADING STATISTICS

The "Racial Justice Act" is based on the misinformed myth that black defendants are sentenced to death more often than white defendants for the same categories of crimes. No study has ever shown this to be the case. In fact, the opposite is true.

As Dr. Stephen Klein, a statistician with Rand Corporation, testified during a hearing before the Subcommittee on Civil and Constitution Rights in July of 1991, a black defendant stands a better chance of avoiding a death sentence for a homicide conviction. This fact is affirmed by data from the Bureau of Justice Statistics, which shows that white homicide defendants are proportionately more likely to be sentenced to death than black homicide defendants.

While it may be true that killers of white victims are more likely to receive the death penalty than killers of blacks, this statistical disparity is easily explained by the presence of mitigating or aggravating factors which account for the differences in sentences.

What the proponents of the Racial Justice Act will not tell you is that, if there is any problem with the present system, it is that black defendants in homicide cases are proportionately less likely to receive the death penalty than their white counterparts. If the "Racial Justice Act" were really designed to remedy this statistical disparity, the solution would be to seek the death penalty in more cases in which black defendants murder black victims.

Unsurprisingly, this is not the solution posed by the Racial Justice Act. Instead the Racial Justice Act would invalidate the

45

capital sentence of any defendant who decided to raise a claim without regard to whether there was any evidence of racial discrimination in his or her case.

UNDUE BURDENS

The Racial Justice Act will in all likelihood put prosecutors in the untenable position of seeking the death penalty against black murderers of black victims in order to improve their statistical data base as the Act compels them to do. The great irony of the Act is that it injects explicit considerations of race into the prosecutor's decision-making process through the use of statistics. The Act makes race the most important factor in the testing of the constitutionality of the criminal justice system.

The most exhaustive study relied upon by proponents of the Racial Justice Act was performed by Professor David Baldus of the University of Iowa. The Baldus study was carefully examined by the United States District Court of the Northern District of Georgia (Atlanta Division) in McCleskey v. Kemp, 580 F.Supp. 338 (1984) and found wanting. Among other findings, the court concluded:

> The petitioner has failed to make out a *prima facie* case of discrimination based either on race of the victim or race of the defendant disparity. There are many reasons; the three most important of which are that the data base is substantially flawed, that even the largest models are not sufficiently predictive, and that the analyses do not compare like cases. — 580 F.Supp at 364, 365.

In short, the conclusion offered by proponents of the Racial Justice Act, that statistical studies prove that racial discrimination "overwhelmingly and consistently" affects capital sentencing decisions is not supported by any study (nor by Professor Baldus' testimony before the District Court). In fact, with respect to the race of the defendant, the Baldus study, which is considered to be the most comprehensive study of this type, shows no effect of the race of the defendant on capital sentences. With respect to the race of the victim, the differences shown by race are not statistically significant – in other words, the results based on race of the victim could easily be the result of chance deviation rather than considerations of race.

Even if the Baldus study or any other study had obtained more

CRUEL AND NOT-SO-UNUSUAL PUNISHMENT

Reprinted with permission from the **Star Tribune**, Minneapolis.

sound results, one must question the very use of a statistical model to measure a process as complex as that found in capital sentencing. The Baldus study attempted to control for 230 variables. It did not take into consideration, however, two very significant variables – the prosecutor's assessment of the strength of the case or the credibility of witnesses.

In sum, the capital sentencing process, with its infinite variables to achieve and individualize justice, seems to defy statistical analysis. As one of the minority witnesses, Dr. Stephen Klein of the Rand Corporation testified at the hearing of the Subcommittee on Civil and Constitutional Rights on the Racial Justice Act:

> Research in this area is highly suspect because of concerns about sample selection bias, important variables that are not studied, and the use of statistical methods that do not account for the complex interactions among variables that the U.S. Supreme Court says must be considered in rendering a verdict in capital cases.

JUSTICE FOR THE INDIVIDUAL

Apart from the flaws in the statistical studies of death penalty sentencing, there are other serious problems with the Racial

NEITHER RACE NOR JUSTICE

The Racial Justice Act is about neither race nor justice but about abolishing the death penalty...its application would have a seriously disparate impact on racial minorities.

No system of justice is worthy of the name unless it requires that individuals receive their due and actually accomplishes that goal. Imposing criminal punishment because of the color of someone's skin rather than because of his actions is unjust. Similarly, imposing punishment by ignoring the individual's actions is unjust. The Racial Justice Act necessarily makes race the central factor in death penalty decisions and ignores the facts and circumstances of individual cases. It is the very antithesis of justice.

"Is 'Racial Justice' an Oxymoron?" **Policy Insights.** May 1994: 1-2.

Justice Act – so serious that the likely result of its enactment would be the abolition of the death penalty in the United States. A prosecutor will be forced to consider the race of the defendant or the race of the victim when deciding to go for a capital sentence. If his or her numbers do not reflect the proper statistical comparison, the Act requires the prosecutor to prove a negative, i.e., that race did not play a part in the capital sentencing process, or have the sentence revoked.

Another problem with the Racial Justice Act is that it offends the notion of individualized justice. The criminal justice process is designed to allow the jury to carefully consider a number of factors – which do not easily lend themselves to statistical quantification. The purpose of individualized justice is to ensure that each defendant has his or her case carefully decided on its own merits – without regard to other defendants. The Racial Justice Act would create a system of statistically proportional justice where the penalty received would depend on one's membership or the membership of one's victim in a particular racial class.

It is absolutely essential to our system of criminal justice that impermissible factors, such as race, do not affect the capital sentencing process. The Constitution guarantees that race shall not be a factor and numerous procedural safeguards have been put in

STRAIGHTENING OUT THE FACTS

The misconception, often buttressed by careless press reporting, is that blacks get the death penalty far more often than whites for the same offenses. Supporters of the Racial Justice Act in the House have swilled up large gobbets of statistics to prove this, but the claim is false nonetheless.

Thus, author Jared Taylor gives the real facts in his pioneer study of race relations, *Paved with Good Intentions*. "White murderers," writes Taylor, citing criminologist William Wilbanks, "no matter whom they kill, are more likely to get the death penalty than black murderers (11.1 percent to 7.3 percent). Furthermore, whites who kill whites are slightly more likely to be on death row than blacks who kill whites. Finally, whites who kill blacks are slightly more likely to be on death row than blacks who kill whites."

Francis, Samuel. "'Racial Justice Act' Is Prescription for Injustice." **Conservative Chronicle.** Copyright 1994. PJB Enterprises, Inc.

place by the United States Supreme Court to ensure that racial bias does not affect the imposition of the death penalty.

During the full Committee consideration, Congressman Bill McCollum offered a substitute amendment, the Equal Justice Act. The purpose of the amendment is to make a strong declaration that race is not an admissible consideration in decisions to seek or impose criminal penalties. The Equal Justice Act will provide effective safeguards against racial discrimination and racial bias in the administration of the death penalty and other penalties; it outlaws statistical tests and racial quotas for the imposition of the death penalty; it makes killing of a victim motivated by racial prejudice or bias an aggravating factor in federal death penalty prosecutions and it expands federal civil rights protection under 18 U.S.C. 241 and 242 to any "person in" a State, Territory or District. The Equal Justice Act will provide protection against racial discrimination without quotas or the imposition of standards which cannot realistically be achieved.

With the Racial Justice Act, death penalty opponents are simply attempting to do indirectly what they have been unable to do directly – abolish the death penalty.

WHAT IS RACE BIAS?

This activity may be used as an individualized study guide for students in libraries and resource centers or as a discussion catalyst in small group and classroom discussions.

Many readers are unaware that written material usually expresses an opinion or bias. The skill to read with insight and understanding requires the ability to detect different kinds of bias. **Political bias, race bias, sex bias, ethnocentric bias** and **religious bias** are five basic kinds of opinions expressed in editorials and literature that attempt to persuade. This activity will focus on **race bias** defined in the glossary below.

Five Kinds of Editorial Opinion or Bias

Sex Bias — the expression of dislike for and/or feeling of superiority over a person because of gender or sexual preference

Race Bias — the expression of dislike for and/or feeling of superiority over a racial group

Ethnocentric Bias — the expression of a belief that one's own group, race, religion, culture or nation is superior. Ethnocentric persons judge others by their own standards and values.

Political Bias — the expression of opinions and attitudes about government-related issues on the local, state, national or international level

Religious Bias — the expression of a religious belief or attitude

Guidelines

Read through the following statements and decide which ones represent **race bias**. Evaluate each statement by using the method indicated below.

- **Mark (R)** for statements that reflect any **race bias**.

- **Mark (O)** for statements that reflect other kinds of opinion or bias.

- **Mark (F)** for any factual statements.

- **Mark (N)** for any statements that you are not sure about.

_____ 1. Murders that occur daily in society demonstrate the need for the death penalty.

_____ 2. The claim of racial discrimination in the death penalty cannot be supported with facts.

_____ 3. The evidence of racial bias in the imposition of the death penalty in the Deep South is shocking.

_____ 4. The death penalty has been used most frequently as a method to punish blacks.

_____ 5. Between the Civil War and the present, African Americans were far more often sentenced to death after conviction of a serious crime than whites.

_____ 6. Most studies show no pattern of evidence indicating racial disparities in the imposition of the death penalty.

_____ 7. Minority populations are more likely to commit violent crimes.

_____ 8. The difference between blacks and whites is not one of degree, but of kind.

_____ 9. Those more educated minority populations are less of a burden to society.

_____ 10. It is possible for whites and blacks to be brothers in Christ without being brothers in law.

_____ 11. Blacks are better athletes than whites.

_____ 12. Asians have proven to be more motivated students than whites.

_____ 13. All races should enjoy the same social privileges and protection.

_____ 14. By nature all races are equal in all things.

Other Activities

1. Locate three examples of *racial* or *ethnic* bias in the readings from Chapter Two.

2. Make up one-sentence statements that would be an example of each of the following: **sex bias, race bias, ethnocentric bias, and religious bias**.

CHAPTER 3

THE DEATH PENALTY AND INNOCENCE

READING

6

THE DANGER OF MISTAKEN EXECUTION

Don Edwards

Congressman Don Edwards, Democrat of California, along with his then majority colleagues Pat Schroeder, Barney Frank, Craig Washington and Jarrold Nadler, issued a staff report on the death penalty and innocence during the 2nd session of the 103rd Congress. The Subcommittee on Civil and Constitutional Rights is part of the Full House Committee on the Judiciary.

■ POINTS TO CONSIDER

1. Summarize why the authors feel that innocence is an issue that needs to be examined, especially with respect to capital punishment.

2. Discuss the ways in which the system fails those erroneously convicted of capital crimes.

3. Contrast the issues surrounding innocence before and after conviction.

4. What kinds of resources outside the judicial system have aided in claims of innocence for those convicted of capital crimes? How effective have they been? How often are they employed?

5. Why do the authors claim that the appellate process hinders persons with claims of innocence? How has the Supreme Court decided on capital challenges based on new evidence of innocence?

Excerpted from a majority staff report of the House of Representatives Subcommittee on Civil and Constitutional Rights of the House Judiciary Committee, November 1994.

Errors can be and have been made repeatedly in the trial of death penalty cases because of poor representation, racial prejudice, prosecutorial misconduct, or simply the presentation of erroneous evidence. Once convicted, a death row inmate faces serious obstacles in convincing any tribunal that he is innocent.

In 1972, when the Supreme Court ruled in Furman v. Georgia that the death penalty as then applied was arbitrary and capricious and therefore unconstitutional, a majority of the Justices expected that the adoption of narrowly crafted sentencing procedures would protect against innocent persons being sentenced to death. Yet the promise of Furman has not been fulfilled: innocent persons are still being sentenced to death, and the chances are high that innocent persons have been or will be executed.

No issue posed by capital punishment is more disturbing to the public than the prospect that the government might execute an innocent person. A recent national poll found that the number one concern raising doubts among voters regarding the death penalty is the danger of a mistaken execution. Fifty-eight percent of voters are disturbed that the death penalty might allow an innocent person to be executed.

The most conclusive evidence that innocent people are condemned to death under modern death sentencing procedures comes from the surprisingly large number of people whose convictions have been overturned and who have been freed from death row. Four former death row inmates have been released from prison just this year after their innocence became apparent: Kirk Bloodsworth, Federico Macias, Walter McMillian, and Gregory Wilhoit.

As of November 1994, at least 52 people have been released from prison after serving time on death row since 1973 with significant evidence of their innocence. In 47 of these cases, the defendant was subsequently acquitted, pardoned, or charges were dropped. In three of the cases, a compromise was reached and the defendants were immediately released upon pleading to a lesser offense. In the remaining two cases, one defendant was released when the parole board became convinced of his innocence, and the other was acquitted at a retrial of the capital charge but convicted of lesser related charges.

55

BREAKDOWN OF THE SYSTEM: RACE, PRESSURE, COUNSEL, MISCONDUCT

These 52 cases illustrate the flaws inherent in the death sentencing systems used in the states. Some of these men were convicted on the basis of perjured testimony or because the prosecutor improperly withheld exculpatory evidence. In other cases, racial prejudice was a determining factor. In others, defense counsel failed to conduct the necessary investigation that would have disclosed exculpatory information.

Sometimes racial prejudice propels an innocent person into the role of despicable convict. In 1980, a 16-year-old white girl named Cheryl Dee Fergeson was raped and murdered at a Texas high school. Suspicion turned to the school's five janitors. One of the janitors later testified that the police looked at Clarence Brandley, the only black in the group, and said, "Since you're the nigger, you're elected."

Brandley was convicted and sentenced to death by an all-white jury after two trials. After six years of fruitless appeals and civil rights demonstrations in support of Brandley, the Texas Court of Criminal Appeals stated that "The court unequivocally concludes that the color of Clarence Brandley's skin was a substantial factor which pervaded all aspects of the State's capital prosecution of him." Brandley was eventually released in 1990 and all charges were dismissed.

In 1986, in the small town of Monroeville, Alabama, an 18-year-old white woman was shot to death and no one was arrested for eight months. On the day of the murder, Walter McMillian was at a fish fry with his friends and relatives. Many of these people gave testimony at trial that McMillian could not have committed the murder of Ronda Morrison because he was with them all day. Nevertheless, he was arrested, tried and convicted of the murder.

The jury in the trial recommended a life sentence for McMillian but the judge overruled this recommendation and sentenced him to death. His case went through four rounds of appeal, all of which were denied. New attorneys, not paid by the State of Alabama, voluntarily took over the case and eventually found that the prosecutors had illegally withheld evidence which would have pointed to McMillian's innocence. Finally, the State agreed to investigate its earlier handling of the case and then admitted that a grave mistake had been made. Mr. McMillian was freed on March 3, 1993.

Federico Macias' court-appointed lawyer did virtually nothing to prepare the case for trial. Macias was sentenced to death in Texas in 1984. Two days before his scheduled execution, Macias received a stay. New counsel from the large Skadden, Arps law firm had entered the case and devoted to it the firm's considerable resources and expertise. Mr. Macias' conviction was overturned via a federal writ of *habeas corpus*, which was upheld by a unanimous panel of the U.S. Court of Appeals for the Fifth Circuit in December, 1992.

While Clarence Chance and Benny Powell were not sentenced to death, their convictions for murder illustrate the dangers of overzealous police work. They were released from prison last year after Jim McCloskey of Centurion Ministries took on their case and demonstrated their innocence. The City of Los Angeles awarded them $7 million, and the judge termed the police department's conduct "reprehensible" while apologizing for the "gross injustices" that occurred.

DESPITE THE SYSTEM

These men were found innocent despite the system and only as a result of extraordinary efforts not generally available to death row defendants.

Indeed, in some cases, these men were found innocent as a result of sheer luck. In the case of Walter McMillian, his volunteer outside counsel had obtained from the prosecutors an audio tape of one of the key witnesses' statements incriminating Mr. McMillian. After listening to the statement, the attorney flipped the tape over to see if anything was on the other side. It was only then that he heard the same witness complaining that he was being pressured to frame Mr. McMillian. With that fortuitous break, the whole case against McMillian began to fall apart.

Most of the releases from death row over the past twenty years came only after many years and many failed appeals. The average length of time between conviction and release was almost seven years for the death row inmates since 1970. Too often, the reviews afforded death row inmates on appeal and *habeas corpus* simply do not offer a meaningful opportunity to present claims of innocence.

In the criminal justice system, defendants are presumed to be innocent until proven guilty beyond a reasonable doubt. Thus, a person is fully entitled to a claim of innocence if charges are not brought against him or if the charges brought are not proven. A person may be guilty of other crimes or there may be some who still insist he is guilty, but with respect to the charge in question, he is innocent.

In the absence of adequate legal mechanisms, the most serious errors in the criminal justice system are sometimes uncovered as a result of such extra-judicial factors as the media and the development of new scientific techniques. These following cases illustrate the randomness of how the legal system works.

One unpredictable element that can affect whether an innocent person is released is the involvement of the media. In Randall Dale Adams' case, film producer Errol Morris went to Texas to make a documentary on Dr. James Grigson, the notorious "Dr. Death." Grigson would claim 100% certainty for his courtroom predictions that a particular defendant would kill again, and he made such a prediction about Randall Adams.

In the course of his investigation of Grigson, Morris became interested in Adams' plight and helped unearth layers of prosecutorial misconduct in that case. He also obtained on tape a virtual confession by another person. Morris' movie, *The Thin Blue Line*, told Randall Adams' story in a way no one had seen before. The movie was released in 1988 and Adams was freed the following year.

Similarly, all charges and death sentences against Thomas Gladish, Richard Greer, Ronald Keine, and Clarence Smith were dropped in 1976 thanks, in part, to the *Detroit News* investigation of lies told by the prosecution's star witness. Walter McMillian's case was featured on *60 Minutes* shortly before his release.

In 1984, a nine-year-old girl named Dawn Hamilton was raped and murdered in Baltimore County, Maryland. No physical evidence linked Kirk Bloodsworth to the crime. He was convicted and sentenced to death because he looked like someone who might have committed the crime.

When a new volunteer lawyer agreed to look into Bloodsworth's case, he decided to try one more time to have the evidence in the case tested. He sent the underwear to a laboratory in California that used newly developed DNA techniques. The defense attorney was astonished when he learned that there was testable DNA material. The tests showed that the semen stain on the underwear could not possibly have come from Mr. Bloodsworth. The prosecution then agreed that if these results could be duplicated by the FBI's crime laboratory, it would consent to Mr. Bloodsworth's release. On Friday, June 25, the FBI's results affirmed what Bloodsworth had been saying all along: he was innocent of all charges. On June 28, he was released by order of the court from the Maryland State Correctional facility in Jessup, after nine years in prison – two of which were on death row.

The trial is obviously the critical time for the defendant to make his or her case for innocence. Unfortunately, the manner in which defense counsel are selected and compensated for death penalty trials does not always protect the defendant's rights at this pivotal time. Most defendants facing the death penalty cannot afford to hire their own attorney, so the state is required to provide them with one. Some states have public defender offices staffed by attorneys trained to handle such cases. In other states, attorneys are appointed from the local community and the quality of representation is spotty. Federico Macias is certainly not alone with respect to ineffective counsel.

Although death penalty law is a highly specialized and complex form of litigation, there is no guarantee that the attorney appointed to this critical role will have the necessary expertise. There is no independent appointing authority to select only qualified counsel for these cases, and attorneys are frequently underpaid and understaffed, with few resources for this critical undertaking.

THE APPELLATE PROCESS

If an innocent defendant is convicted, he generally has little time to collect and present new evidence which might reverse his conviction. All death row inmates are assured representation to make one direct appeal in their state courts. If that appeal is denied, representation is no longer assured.

When someone has been unjustly convicted under circumstances similar to those described above, he can challenge that conviction in federal court through the writ of *habeas corpus*. Although numerous legislative proposals to limit *habeas corpus* in the past few years have failed, the opportunity for using this writ has already been stringently narrowed by recent Supreme Court decisions.

The Supreme Court has denied *habeas* review of claims from prisoners on death row with persuasive, newly discovered evidence of their innocence. Death row inmates who claim their innocence are therefore often forced to rely on procedural claims. But those, too, are being foreclosed by the Supreme Court.

A recent narrowing of the writ requires federal courts to reject all claims if the proper procedures were not followed by the defendant in state court. Roger Coleman, for example, filed his Virginia State appeal three days late, and this error by his attorneys barred any consideration of his federal constitutional claims.

For the innocent defendant, the last avenue of relief is clemency from the executive branch. All death penalty states have some form of pardon power vested in either the governor or in a board of review. However, clemencies in death penalty cases are extremely rare. Since the death penalty was re-instated in 1976, 4,800 death sentences have been imposed but less than three dozen clemencies have been granted on defendants' petitions.

CONCLUSION

Americans are justifiably concerned about the possibility that an innocent person may be executed. Errors can be and have been made repeatedly in the trial of death penalty cases because of poor representation, racial prejudice, prosecutorial misconduct, or simply the presentation of erroneous evidence. Once convicted, a death row inmate faces serious obstacles in convincing any tribunal that he is innocent.

Once an execution occurs, the small group of lawyers who handle post-conviction proceedings in death penalty cases in the United States move on to the next crisis. Investigation of innocence ends after execution. If an innocent person was among the 222 people executed in the United States since Furman, nobody in the legal system is any longer paying attention.

Many death penalty convictions and sentences are overturned on appeal, but too frequently the discovery of error is the result of finding expert appellate counsel, a sympathetic judge willing to waive procedural barriers, and a compelling set of facts which can overcome the presumption of guilt. Not all of the convicted death row inmates are likely to have these opportunities.

READING

7

THE RARE CHANCE OF MISTAKEN EXECUTION

Paul G. Cassell

Paul G. Cassell delivered this statement in his capacity as Associate Professor of Law at the University of Utah College of Law. His background in criminal justice includes positions as Assistant U.S. Attorney General in the Eastern District of VA and Associate Deputy Attorney General in the U.S. Department of Justice. He has published numerous pieces on the topic of mistaken execution.

■ POINTS TO CONSIDER

1. Explain the term "mistaken commutation." Why is this considered a more serious problem by the author than risk of executing an innocent? What evidence does he provide?

2. Summarize the deterrent effect of the death penalty according to the author.

3. Discuss the safeguards present in the criminal justice system which aid in capital prisoners' claims of actual innocence. Contrast the safeguards outlined in this article with the concerns about innocence claims and the criminal justice system in the previous article.

Excerpted from the testimony of Paul G. Cassell before the Subcommittee on Civil and Constitutional Rights of the House Judiciary Committee, July 23, 1993.

No innocent person has been executed in recent history; the failure to impose death penalties can result – and has resulted – in the death of innocent persons.

Mistakes in capital cases fall into two categories. On the one hand, it is possible that an innocent person might be executed. It is the specter of this kind of error that opponents of the death penalty apparently seek to raise before this Committee. But it is also possible to make quite a different kind of mistake in capital cases. A guilty capital murderer might be spared the ultimate penalty only to kill other innocent persons. The risk to innocent life from failing to carry out capital sentences imposed under contemporary safeguards far outweighs the speculative and remote risk that an execution might be in error.

NO MISTAKEN EXECUTIONS HAVE OCCURRED IN RECENT HISTORY

Given the fallibility of human judgments, the possibility exists that the use of capital punishment may result in the execution of an innocent person. The Senate Judiciary Committee has previously found this risk to be "minimal," a view shared by numerous scholars. As Justice Powell has noted commenting on the numerous state capital cases that have come before the Supreme Court, the "unprecedented safeguards" already inherent in capital sentencing statutes "ensure a degree of care in the imposition of the sentence of death that can only be described as unique."

While the widely-held view has been that state death penalties are imposed with extraordinary care and accuracy, that position has recently been challenged. In 1987, two avowed opponents of capital punishment, Professors Hugo Adam Bedau and Michael L. Radelet, published the results of what they claimed to be "sustained and systematic" research over many years purporting to show that the use of capital punishment entails an intolerable risk of mistaken executions of defendants who are factually innocent of the crimes for which they were convicted.

In 1988 after extensive research, then-Assistant Attorney General Stephen J. Markman and I published in the *Stanford Law Review* a detailed rebuttal to the assertions of Bedau and Radelet. We agreed with Bedau and Radelet that the execution of even one innocent person would be a tragedy. But we concluded that "not only is the Bedau-Radelet study severely flawed in critical respects, but it wholly fails to demonstrate an unacceptable risk of executing the innocent. To the contrary, it confirms – as convincingly as may be possible – the view that the risk is too small to be a significant factor in the debate over the death penalty." The overwhelming majority of Americans who support capital punishment can rest assured that the criminal justice system is doing an admirable, if not indeed perfect, job of preventing the execution of innocent defendants.

MISTAKEN COMMUTATIONS OF DEATH SENTENCES

While modern-day examples of executed innocent defendants remain as rare as unicorns, it is much easier to find evidence that failure to execute justly convicted capital murderers would produce fatal mistakes, mistakes that I will designate as "mistaken commutations." Capital punishment saves innocent lives in three ways: through its incapacitative effect, its deterrent effect, and its role in establishing a system of just punishment. Failure to carry out properly imposed death sentences, after reasonable judicial and executive review, would thus be a mistake with consequences no less lethal than a mistaken execution.

Let me emphasize that I am not urging that every first degree murderer be executed lest he kill again. Our present system of capital punishment limits the ultimate penalty to certain specifically-defined crimes and even then, permits the penalty of death only when the jury finds that the aggravating circumstances in the case outweigh all mitigating circumstances. The system further provides judicial review of capital cases. Finally, before capital sentences are carried out, the governor or other executive official will review the sentence to insure that it is a just one, a determination that undoubtedly considers the evidence of the condemned defendant's guilt. Once all of those decision-makers have agreed that a death sentence is appropriate, innocent lives would be lost from failure to impose the sentence.

INCAPACITATION

Capital sentences, when carried out, save innocent lives by permanently incapacitating murderers. Some persons who commit capital homicide will slay other innocent persons if given the opportunity to do so. The death penalty is the most effective means of preventing such killers from repeating their crimes. The next most serious penalty, life imprisonment without possibility of parole, prevents murderers from committing some crimes but does not prevent them from murdering in prison. At least five federal prison officers have been killed since December 1982, and the inmates in at least three of the incidents were already serving life sentences for murder.

Some killers are also paroled, only to kill again. For instance, Eddie Simon Wein was sentenced to death in Los Angeles Superior Court in 1957. Instead of being executed, he was released from prison in 1975 to live in West Los Angeles. Within months, he began to attack and kill women in the area.

NOT AN ISOLATED EXAMPLE

Out of a sample of 164 paroled Georgia murderers, eight committed subsequent murders within seven years of release. A study of twenty Oregon murderers released on parole in 1979 found that one (i.e., five percent) had committed a subsequent homicide within five years of release. Another study found that of 11,404 persons originally convicted of "willful homicide" and released during 1965 and 1974, 34 were returned to prison for commission of a subsequent criminal homicide during the first year alone. Of course, these figures reflect recidivism by murderers in general, not the presumptively more dangerous population of capital murderers.

While it is impossible to determine precisely how many innocent lives the execution of convicted murderers has saved, the available data suggest that the number is not insignificant. Of the roughly 52,000 state prison inmates serving time for murder in 1984, an estimated 810 had previously been convicted of murder and had killed 821 persons following those convictions. Execution of each of these inmates following their initial murder conviction would have saved 821 innocent lives. Of course, since only a fraction of convicted murderers receive the death penalty, the number of innocent lives would be substantially smaller. Our data published in 1988 suggest a conservative estimate of at least 24 innocent lives saved just in the last few decades from the incapacitative effect of capital sentences, more than the total number of "innocent" defendants that Bedau and Radelet claim have been executed in this century.

DETERRENCE

While the innocent lives saved through the incapacitative effect of capital punishment are important, the penalty also saves far more innocent lives through its general deterrent effect. Support for the deterrent effect of the death penalty comes from four sources: logic, anecdotal evidence, deterrence studies, and the structure of our criminal penalties.

Logic supports the conclusion that the death penalty is the most effective deterrent for some kinds of murders – those that require reflection and forethought by persons of reasonable intelligence and unimpaired mental facilities.

Anecdotal evidence in support of the deterrent value of capital sentences comes from examples of persons who have been deterred from murdering, or risking a murder, because of the death penalty. For instance, Justice McComb of the California Supreme Court collected from the files of the Los Angeles Police Department fourteen examples within a four-year period of defendants who, in explaining their refusal to take a life or carry a weapon, pointed to the presence of the death penalty.

Statistical studies support the proposition that capital sentences, like other criminal sanctions, have a deterrent effect. To be sure, some statistical surveys, often conducted by opponents of the death penalty, have found no such effect.

One of the most recent substantial econometric studies was performed by Professor Stephen K. Layson of the University of North Carolina at Greensboro, who analyzed data for the United States from 1936 to 1977. Layson concluded that increases in the probability of execution reduced the homicide rate. Specifically, Layson found that, on average, each execution deterred approximately eighteen murders.

Indeed, the premise that more severe penalties deter crimes is fundamental to our criminal justice system. This Committee, for example, has often responded to the problem of crime by proposing new legislation that would increase the severity of criminal sanctions for certain criminal activities. Penalties for drug trafficking and firearms offenses immediately come to mind here. If those enhanced penalties were appropriate because they would help deter those offenses, death penalties for homicides are likewise appropriate because they will deter some would-be killers.

If Layson's empirical work (which is strongly supported by our intuition, anecdotal evidence, deterrence theory, and the structure of our criminal penalties) is correct, the death penalty has deterred roughly 125,000 murders in this country in this century.

JUST PUNISHMENT

Certain crimes constitute such outrageous violation of human and moral values that they demand retribution. It was to control the natural human impulse and to seek revenge and, more broadly, to give expression to deeply held views that some conduct deserves punishment, that criminal laws, administered by the State, were established.

CURRENT SAFEGUARDS AGAINST AN ERRONEOUS EXECUTION

The preceding sections have demonstrated two points: first, that no innocent person has been executed in recent history; and, second, the failure to impose death penalties can result – and has resulted – in the death of innocent persons. This section briefly reviews the current accommodation that has been reached between the need to review claims of innocence while at the same time allowing the effective imposition of death penalties.

67

The current capital sentencing scheme guards against the execution of innocent persons in at least seven ways.

First, the system imposes a vast array of due process protections to assure that no innocent person is convicted of a crime.

Second, with respect to the role of federal courts in the process, federal courts can review the sufficiency of the evidence supporting a guilty verdict to ensure that the evidence was sufficient to persuade a rational trier of fact beyond a reasonable doubt of every element of the charged offense.

Third, the federal courts will allow any prisoner who can demonstrate his "actual innocence" to seek relief under federal *habeas* for a procedural error at this trial, even if the prisoner has forfeited his right to seek relief on *habeas corpus* due to a procedural default in the state courts or an abuse of the writ.

Fourth, prosecutorial misconduct will result in reversal of a conviction. Both federal and state prosecutors are constitutionally required to disclose exculpatory evidence to a defendant and impeaching information regarding government witnesses. Failure to disclose such information that is material to a defendant's case requires a new trial. Moreover, a prosecutor may not knowingly present false testimony and, indeed, has a duty to correct testimony known as false. Thus, if government misconduct results in the conviction of an innocent person, a remedy already exists.

Fifth, in the event that evidence comes to light after a trial that casts doubt on the accuracy of the trial verdict, a defendant may file a motion for a new trial. For example, in the federal system, Rule 33 of the Federal Rules of Criminal Procedure allows a defendant to file a motion for a new trial based on newly discovered evidence within two years of trial. All fifty states and the District of Columbia authorize motions for new trials based on newly discovered evidence, with time limits ranging from ten days after judgment to no time limits at all.

In the event that exculpatory evidence is discovered after the time limits have expired, the **sixth** – and perhaps most important – safeguard against the execution of an innocent person is the possibility of clemency. It is even possible that executive clemency can come in the form of a motion by the prosecutor involved in the case. It seems likely that any prosecutors would drop charges in a case of genuine proof of a defendant's innocence.

On top of all of these safeguards, the United States Supreme Court has recently recognized the possibility of even another, **seventh** safeguard against erroneous executions: review of claims of innocence on federal *habeas*. The Supreme Court cast doubt on the vitality of this limitation and suggested that claims of innocence could be reviewed on federal *habeas* in extraordinary circumstances. In Herrera v. Collins, the Court reviewed a claim raised by petitioner Herrera that he was actually innocent of the capital murder. In various opinions, the Court denied his claim in a six-to-three decision. Of importance for present purposes, however, is that six Justices suggested that a sufficiently persuasive claim of actual innocence would entitle a petitioner to federal *habeas* relief. The opinion for the Court, written by Chief Justice Rehnquist, did not deny Herrera's contention that executing an innocent man would be subject to federal *habeas* review. Instead, the Court chose to "assume, for the sake of argument in deciding this case, that in a capital case a truly persuasive demonstration of 'actual innocence' made after trial would render the execution of a defendant unconstitutional." The three dissenters (Justices Blackmun, Stevens, and Souter) went further, and would allow a prisoner to raise a claim on *habeas* if he could establish that he "probably is innocent."

In sum, the current capital sentencing scheme has an extraordinary array of safeguards to prevent the execution of an innocent person.

READING

8

THE HORROR OF MISTAKEN EXECUTION

Michael L. Radelet, Hugo Adam Bedau and Constance E. Putnam

Michael L. Radelet is Associate Professor of Sociology at the University of Florida and the editor of Facing the Death Penalty. *Hugo Adam Bedau is Austin Fletcher Professor of Philosophy at Tufts University. He is editor of* The Death Penalty in America *and of* Death Is Different, *published by Northeastern University Press. Constance E. Putnam is a Boston-area writer who has published numerous articles on a variety of social issues.*

■ POINTS TO CONSIDER

1. According to the authors' research, discuss the problem of executing innocents in this century.

2. How do the authors respond to critics of their research?

3. Analyze the difficulties in evaluating claims of innocence.

4. How has history played a role in the authors' view of capital punishment?

In the United States not only do countless men and women get arrested for murders they did not commit – they get convicted and often sentenced to death as well. Occasionally they are even executed, and we document twenty-three such cases...

The rest of the stories – nearly four hundred – are those of the lucky defendants. They are the ones whose innocence was eventually established so convincingly that the State finally did, in one way or another, admit its errors and correct them. And 150 or so of those who were once wrongly under sentence of death did at least escape execution, their death sentences for a variety of reasons having been nullified before the ultimate tragedy occurred. Often, as we have seen, it was fickle good fortune rather than anything having to do with the rational workings of the criminal justice system that played the crucial role in sparing these innocent defendants. Yet luck was not sufficient to spare them time in prison (often many years), the agony of uncertainty over whether they would ever be vindicated and released, and blighted hopes for a decent life all too frequently destroyed by the ordeal and stigma of a murder conviction. There are more cases that will probably never be documented in which innocent individuals were executed before they were able to prove their innocence. As Voltaire argued in the eighteenth century and Bentham in the nineteenth, we argue in the twentieth century that the risk of executing the innocent is and will remain one of the strongest objections to capital punishment.

ADDRESSING THE SKEPTICS

Defenders of the death penalty have responded to this objection in two ways. Some want to challenge our research and the adequacy of the evidence we cite in support of the twenty-three cases where we believe an innocent person was executed. Reasonable and unbiased judges, they claim, would not be persuaded by the evidence that has persuaded us. These critics remind us that no court, chief executive, or other official body has ever acknowledged that an innocent person has been executed in this century – as if that constituted evidence that it has never happened. Other critics are willing to concede, at least for the sake of argument, that some two dozen erroneous executions may have occurred, but they insist that this is a small price to pay for the benefits they claim the death penalty provides. They further argue that reasonable people would no more abolish the death penalty because of the risk of fatal error than they would outlaw truck driving because of the risk of fatal accidents.

Both these objections deserve serious thought and a considered reply. In regard to the initial objection, we would grant that more research is desirable regarding the cases of wrongful execution that we cite; we would welcome the interest of other scholars, journalists, writers, and civil rights advocates in re-opening all these cases to public scrutiny. Unfortunately, much of the further research that needs to be done is likely to prove inconclusive or impossible to carry out. More often than not, the important witnesses and other participants in the case are dead, and the relevant physical evidence has long ago vanished or been destroyed. Future research efforts might very well leave us no better informed than we are now.

Our investigations lead us to believe that the small number of cases we have identified in which an innocent person was executed is an indication not of the fairness of the system but rather of its finality. Very few death penalty cases in this century have attracted the sustained interest of persons in a position to undertake the research necessary to challenge successfully a guilty verdict meted out to a defendant later executed; funds are rarely available to investigate execution of the allegedly innocent (there are not even adequate funds available to investigate thoroughly those in prison who claim to be innocent).

THE CHALLENGE OF VALIDATING INNOCENCE CLAIMS

Once the defendant is dead, the best source of evidence is gone. So is the primary motive for re-investigating the case. Further, the limited resources of the defense lawyers (the ones in the best position to direct additional investigations into their deceased client's guilt or innocence) are quickly absorbed by the legal battles to save the lives of others still on death row. The result is that, as time passes, the possibility of continuing an effective investigation slowly disappears.

Neither is there now (nor has there ever been) any organization whose purpose is to gather and sift the evidence for a defendant's possible innocence after that defendant has been executed. The best-known previous investigators of wrongful convictions – Yale law professor Edwin Borchard; federal judge Jerome Frank and his

72

attorney-daughter, Barbara; journalists Edward Radin and Eugene Block – worked essentially alone and ignored the claims to innocence of those already executed. Erle Stanley Gardner's Court of Last Resort did a remarkable job of investigating a few capital cases, and our Inventory is indebted to its labors. But we know of no instance where the Court attempted to re-open any case of allegedly erroneous execution. Moreover, that organization was in business less than two decades, and it never confined its attention to defendants under a death sentence. Centurion Ministries, founded in 1981 by James McCloskey, has helped free many innocent prisoners – including one on death row. But it understandably devotes none of its slender resources to investigating a case after a prisoner has been executed.

As if these difficulties were not enough, no matter how much evidence we might gather concerning a given case, there is simply no tribunal before which it can be placed and from which an authoritative posthumous judgment can be rendered on the innocence of an executed convict. Bluntly put, there is no forum for hearing the case for innocence of someone already dead. We are necessarily confined to less formal methods and procedures, whose adequacy can always be challenged by the skeptic.

As for the fact that responsible officials have never publicly acknowledged that an innocent person has been lawfully executed, we do not think their silence ought to be taken as evidence that the system makes no fatal errors. Those involved in pressing a death penalty case from arrest to execution, whether private citizens or government officials, not surprisingly tend to close ranks and resist admission of error. More distressingly, they have been known to obstruct others even from exploring charges of erroneous execution – as every serious investigator of wrongful convictions has pointed out...

EVIDENCE FOR DOUBT

Finally, if one concedes (as any fair-minded reader must) that there have been hundreds of innocent persons wrongly convicted of murder, then it seems strange and implausible to insist that the evidence is wholly insufficient to show that even one innocent person has ever been executed in the United States during this century. Are we to believe that although hundreds of demonstrably innocent persons have been erroneously imprisoned, not even one has been wrongfully executed? Surely there is nothing about

73

the penalty of death and the way it is administered to make us sanguine on this point, nothing to ensure that the innocent have never been and will never be executed. On the contrary, it seems to us a virtual certainty that some, perhaps many, innocent persons – one can only speculate on the exact number – have been executed, just as hundreds have been imprisoned.

One cornerstone of this judgment is to be found in the more than two dozen cases we have identified where at the very last – days, hours, or minutes prior to execution – a reprieve or stay saved the life of a prisoner later exonerated...We reported the case of Isidore Zimmerman, saved within two hours of electrocution...We related the story of Lloyd Miller, spared from execution seven times – including once when he was just seven hours from death. These cases are not unique; we know of twenty-five more, all reported in our Inventory of Cases. Among them are the following:

In 1932 in North Carolina, Gus Langley had his head shaved ready for electrocution when a technical error in his death sentence was discovered that stayed the execution. Later, new evidence proved that his alibi was legitimate.

In 1942 in North Carolina, William Wellman was seated in the electric chair when the governor, having just learned that another man had confessed, issued a reprieve.

In 1957 in Ohio, Harry Bundy was only three days from execution when a witness to the crime chanced to read about the case, notified the authorities, and secured a stay of the execution. As the Columbus, Ohio, newspaper observed, "It was sheer luck that saved Harry Bundy from execution."

In 1983 Joseph Green Brown came within thirteen hours of electrocution in Florida before a federal district court judge granted a stay of execution. Three years later, his conviction was vacated by the Eleventh Circuit Court of Appeals when it was discovered that the prosecution had used perjured testimony to obtain the conviction. All charges against Brown were then dropped.

That same year, also in Florida, half-brothers William Jent and Earnest Miller came within sixteen hours of sitting in the electric chair. As in Brown's case, the convictions were later vacated in federal court. This time the reason was the discovery that the prosecution had suppressed exculpatory evidence.

74

Jent and Miller and the others mentioned here were not the only lucky ones. But can anyone seriously believe that all innocent murder convicts sentenced to death have been equally lucky?

TOO HIGH A PRICE

The second response death penalty advocates make to our claim that innocents have been executed concedes that terrible errors have occurred – and will occur again – but argues that this is a price worth paying. Our reply to this objection rests on two considerations. First, there is only the weakest possible analogy between a state-imposed system of capital punishment, and risky but lawful practices such as undersea exploration, skydiving, mining, and the ordinary operation of motor vehicles. In all these activities, innocent people are occasionally killed. But although no one engaging in them behaves in an intentionally lethal manner toward anyone, the death penalty is deliberately – and inherently – lethal. None of the activities mentioned above coerces its participants; the death penalty most assuredly does coerce. Interfering with skydiving or mining by prohibiting it under law would constitute an unreasonable interference with voluntary behavior (and on unacceptable paternalistic grounds). Abolishing the death penalty would interfere with no one's liberty...

A TAINTED HISTORY

The history of capital punishment in western civilization might well be said to have begun with the execution of the innocent – Socrates in Athens in 399 B.C. and Jesus in Jerusalem in A.D. 30. In the centuries from those days to the present, countless others who were innocent have been put to death. Most were not famous; their names, if remembered at all, are known but to a few. Just a century ago, Illinois executed three of the Haymarket anarchists – August Spies, Adolph Fischer, and George Engel – only to have them all later exonerated by Governor Altgeld (one of the rare instances in any century that such an error has been officially admitted). What errors of the same sort in our time will historians record a century from now?

EXECUTION OF INNOCENTS IS AN UNFOUNDED FEAR

Stephen Markman

Stephen Markman is a Detroit lawyer. He served as Assistant Attorney General of the United States for legal policy during the Reagan Administration.

■ **POINTS TO CONSIDER**

1. Why is Markman critical of Justice Blackmun's final dissent? How does this dissent differ from Blackmun's past view of the constitutionality of the death penalty?

2. Discuss Markman's criticisms with regard to the Radelet/Bedau research. Give specific examples.

3. What motivation does the author suggest lies behind research of erroneous execution? Does the author give legitimacy to any arguments against the death penalty?

Excerpts from "Innocents on Death Row?" by Stephen Markman, **National Review**, Sept. 12, 1994, pp. 72-79, 92. © 1994 by NATIONAL REVIEW, Inc., 150 East 35th Street, New York, NY 10016. Reprinted by permission.

Most inveterate opponents of capital punishment are not influenced by whether or not it is administered in a "reliable" fashion.

In announcing earlier this year that he would "no longer tinker with the machinery of death" by voting to sustain capital punishment, Justice Harry Blackmun relied not only upon an understanding of the Constitution informed more by his own curious conscience than by the text or history of that document, but also upon his belief that "innocent persons have been executed...and will continue to be executed under our death penalty scheme."

In making this assertion, Justice Blackmun cited a study published several years ago in the *Stanford Law Review* by two long-time opponents of capital punishment, Hugo Bedau and Michael Radelet. The authors purported to identify "350 cases in which defendants convicted of capital or potentially capital crimes in this century, and in many cases sentenced to death, have later been found to be innocent." This finding was widely heralded in national press releases issued by the American Civil Liberties Union.

Indeed, the Bedau-Radelet study is remarkable not (as Justice Blackmun seems to believe) for demonstrating that mistakes involving the death penalty are common, but rather for demonstrating how uncommon they are. Indeed, to make the finer point, this study – the most thorough and painstaking analysis ever on the subject – fails to prove that a single such mistake has occurred in the United States during this century.

WHERE IS THE EVIDENCE?

One cannot state categorically that mistakes never have been made, but the burden properly belongs with those who have endorsed the proposition that innocent persons have been executed with some degree of regularity in this country. Such a burden lies with Justice Blackmun and his allies because in every capital case a unanimous jury of 12 citizens concluded beyond a reasonable doubt that an individual had committed a capital crime, usually first-degree murder. Further, in every one of these cases a trial judge and an assortment of appellate judges concluded both that the trial was fair and that the 12 jurors had acted reasonably in their determination. While such procedures do not give ironclad assurances that innocent people have not been convicted, they place the burden of proof squarely upon the opposition.

Only 200 of the allegedly wrongful convictions in the Bedau-Radelet study involve first-degree murders in which capital punishment was an option, and in only 139 of these 200 cases were the defendants actually sentenced to death. In only 23 of these 139 cases were the death sentences actually carried out.

So, if there were wrongful executions, it is with regard to these 23 cases, not with regard to those cases in which, as Bedau and Radelet put it, "factors" occurred to prevent the execution of allegedly innocent people.

GUILTY AFTER ALL?

Examination of individual cases cited by the authors will only confirm the reasonableness of the jury's verdict to at least some "neutral observers." In the case of Everett Applegate, executed for murdering his wife with rat poison in 1938, the authors claim that he was innocent because "virtually no evidence against him existed beyond [a co-defendant's] unsupported word." Even if that were true, which it is not, it would not compel the conclusion that Applegate was innocent. Additional evidence, however, was supplied at trial relating to Applegate's motives for killing his wife (his desire to marry another woman and his wife's intention to disclose to authorities information about his continuing sexual relations with a minor), his purchase of rat poison at a drugstore the night of the murder, his admission that he had given his wife that evening considerable amounts of eggnog which happened to be poisoned, and his refusal to consent to an autopsy on his wife.

In the case of Sie Dawson, convicted of murdering a two-year-old child in 1964, Bedau and Radelet base their characterization of his execution as erroneous upon the fact that "years later, newspaper stories revived doubts that had surrounded the conviction from the beginning." However, Dawson had provided a written confession to the police only after learning that an eyewitness was alive; he had repeated the confession 12 days later; the confession was corroborated in its details by independent evidence from other witnesses; and an eyewitness to the crime – the four-year-old brother of the victim, who had been left for dead – told his father and police that Dawson was the one who had killed his brother.

Cartoon by Steve Kelly. Reprinted with permission of *Coply News Service.*

Several of the cases suggest an analysis motivated more strongly by ideology than by a commitment to following the evidence wherever it might lead. In the case of the legendary union organizer Joe Hill, executed in 1915 for shooting a shopkeeper, Bedau and Radelet cite a work of fiction – an "act of imagination," in their words – to support their conclusion that Hill was not guilty. This, despite eyewitness testimony that linked Hill to the crime, evidence that he sought medical attention for a fresh bullet wound the evening of the murder, evidence that the bullet was of the same type as that fired by the victim at his assailant, evidence that Hill asked his doctor not to reveal his wound, and an admission by Hill that he had discarded a gun shortly after leaving the doctor.

NOT INFALLIBLE, BUT...

After "sustained and systematic" research, Bedau and Radelet have pointed to 23 out of more than 7,000 executions during the twentieth century in the United States which they believe to have been erroneous. Presumably, these would be among the most compelling cases for the authors' proposition. Yet in each of the cases where there is a record to review, there are eyewitnesses,

79

RESPONDING TO THE BLACKMUN DISSENT

Convictions in opposition to the death penalty are often passionate and deeply held. That would be no excuse for reading them into a Constitution that does not contain them, even if they represented the convictions of a majority of Americans. Much less is there any excuse for using that course to thrust a minority's views upon the people. Justice Blackmun begins his statement by describing with poignancy the death of a convicted murderer by lethal injection. He chooses, as the case with which to make that statement, one of the less brutal of the murders that regularly come before us – the murder of a man ripped by a bullet suddenly and unexpectedly, with no opportunity to prepare himself and his affairs, and left to bleed to death on the floor of a tavern. The death-by-injection which Justice Blackmun describes looks pretty desirable next to that. It looks even better next to some of the other cases currently before us which Justice Blackmun did not select as the vehicle for his announcement that the death penalty is always unconstitutional – for example, the case of the 11-year-old girl raped by four men and then killed by stuffing her panties down her throat. How enviable a quiet death by lethal injection compared with that! If the people conclude that such more brutal deaths may be deterred by capital punishment; indeed, if they merely conclude that justice requires such brutal deaths to be avenged by capital punishment; the creation of false, untextual and unhistorical contradictions within "the Court's Eighth Amendment jurisprudence" should not prevent them.

Excerpted from the separate majority opinion denying petition of *certiorari* of Justice Antonin Scalia in Callins v. Collins (1994), 127 L Ed 2d 436.

confessions, physical evidence, and circumstantial evidence in support of the defendant's guilt. The authors' claims that the defendants were later "found" or "proven" to be innocent are utterly unpersuasive.

Concededly, it can be a difficult task to raise reasonable doubts about guilt in long-forgotten cases, let alone to prove innocence. However, it is Bedau and Radelet who argue that existing law should be changed because of an identifiable harm; accordingly,

PAIN OF THE VICTIMS

I have been working in this victims' movement for about 14 years, but I know of a lot of people that have stood trial. There is no doubt about it; they were guilty, but they were acquitted. That victim had no appeal, no appeal whatsoever. Now, is that justice?

I believe on the scales of justice that the defendant has far more rights than I do as a victim. I believe it so strongly that I gave up a career in banking to start the victims' movement because my pain was so great, and I saw the injustices, too.

Excerpted from the testimony of Miriam Shehane, VOCAL victims' advocacy group, before the United States Senate Judiciary Committee, April 1, 1993.

they bear the burden of producing credible evidence that the harm exists. It is hard to imagine their evidence satisfying such a burden, except for Justice Blackmun.

None of this is to deny the legitimacy of arguments against the death penalty predicated upon moral opposition. Yet these arguments are not at the core of what either Bedau and Radelet or Justice Blackmun argues.

While the most inveterate opponents of capital punishment are not influenced by whether or not it is administered in a "reliable" fashion, Bedau and Radelet sought to develop a broader base of opposition to the death penalty. Justice Blackmun, who in the past did not join his former colleagues William Brennan and Thurgood Marshall in moral opposition to capital punishment under all circumstances, reflects this intended audience. Those who look at the Bedau-Radelet study with an open mind, however will see that it speaks eloquently about the extraordinary rarity of error in capital punishment.

READING

10

STATE COURTS AND CAPITAL DEFENDANTS: THE POINT

Bryan A. Stevenson

Bryan A. Stevenson is an attorney and Executive Director of the Alabama Capital Representation Center, a private nonprofit organization that provides legal assistance to death row prisoners in Alabama. Prior to his position at the Center, Stevenson served as a staff attorney with the Southern Center for Human Rights in Atlanta.

■ POINTS TO CONSIDER

1. Discuss the author's characterization of the State in the prosecution and conviction of Walter McMillian.

2. Why was it so difficult, according to the author, to establish the innocence of Walter McMillian? What concerns does this raise about indigents on death row?

3. What purpose does telling the story of Walter McMillian serve? Does any greater significance to this story exist with respect to the issue of death penalty and innocence? Why or why not? Explain.

Excerpted from the testimony of Bryan A. Stevenson before the Senate Judiciary Committee, April 1, 1993.

Even after the State's only other witnesses both admitted to State investigators their trial testimony against McMillian was false, the State still refused to acknowledge Mr. McMillian's innocence.

In 1988, I initiated an effort to improve post-conviction litigation in Alabama and agreed to take on appeals for recently sentenced death row prisoners who were indigent and requesting legal assistance. Walter McMillian was one of four cases that I took as we started this initiative in the fall of 1988 involving death row prisoners who had no funds to pay for legal representation but needed immediate legal assistance. Mr. McMillian had been convicted of capital murder on August 17, 1988, for the 1986 murder of Ronda Morrison in Monroeville, Alabama. He was later sentenced to death by Monroe County Circuit Court Judge Robert E. Lee Key, Jr. on September 19, 1988. Judge Key sentenced Mr. McMillian to death despite the fact that the jury had returned a verdict of life imprisonment without parole. Alabama is one of only three states that has permitted trial judges to reject a jury's sentencing verdict and impose the death penalty in a capital case.

Mr. McMillian was a 45-year-old pulp wood worker with no prior felony criminal convictions. After his arrest in June of 1987 for this offense, he spent 14 months in custody awaiting trial after the State moved for postponements of his trial. This kind of delay between arrest and trial is not unusual for indigent defendants, and most capital defendants in Alabama are not tried within a year of their arrest. However, what was unusual about Mr. McMillian's situation was the fact that he spent 13 of the 14 months he awaited trial on Alabama's death row. I had never previously represented anyone who had been sent to death row before being tried, convicted or sentenced.

THE TRIAL

When reviewing Mr. McMillian's trial record after it was completed in 1989, I was immediately struck by the perfunctory nature of the trial court proceedings. Mr. McMillian received a two-day capital murder trial. The trial began at 1:15 p.m. on Monday, August 15, 1988, and was completed by 1:52 pm. on Wednesday, August 17. The penalty phase of Mr. McMillian's trial was conducted in less than two hours. Jury selection, which in many jurisdictions takes days and can, in serious or complex cases, take weeks, began at 9:00 in the morning on the 15th of August and was completed by noon.

QUESTIONABLE EVIDENCE

At Mr. McMillian's trial the State advanced no credible motive for the crime and presented no physical or forensic evidence linking Mr. McMillian to the murder. The State's case against Mr. McMillian turned entirely on the testimony of an alleged white accomplice named Ralph Myers, who had several prior felony convictions and another capital murder case pending against him at the time.

The State also presented testimony from two additional witnesses. Bill Hooks testified that he drove past the cleaners on the morning that Ronda Morrison was murdered and saw Mr. McMillian's truck parked outside the cleaners. Although Ralph Myers had testified that the truck was some fifty yards away from the cleaners in another parking lot, Hooks' testimony was presented by the State as corroborative evidence. Hooks gave his statement to the police while he was in jail on a burglary charge. Immediately after giving this statement to the police, he was released from jail, had fines that he owned the City of Monroeville dismissed at the request of the district attorney and law enforcement officials, and was permitted to avoid payment of fines on subsequent traffic offenses. Hooks was given money by the Sheriff before his testimony and ultimately was paid $5000 in reward money.

A week before Mr. McMillian's trial, another alleged witness, a white man named Joe Hightower, came forward and stated that he also saw Mr. McMillian's truck in front of the cleaners. Mr. Hightower received at least $2000 in reward money. Both men testified at trial that they knew the truck belonged to Mr. McMillian because it was a "low-rider" or that it had been modified to sit close to the ground. While Mr. McMillian owned a low-rider truck at the time of his arrest, his truck was not modified until May of 1987. At the time of the crime in November 1986, his truck was not a low-rider.

On the morning of the crime, Mr. McMillian was at home working on his truck. He and a friend had completely removed his transmission and worked on the truck all morning and until early afternoon. His sister, Evelene Smith, had also organized a fish-fry,

Eleanor Mill sketch

an event where fish and other fried foods were sold to people driving by Mr. McMillian's home to raise money for her church. Several people who were assisting in the fish-fry, people who stopped by Mr. McMillian's home to buy fish, and the man who assisted Mr. McMillian in working on his truck all testified that there was no way he could have been involved in the murder of Ronda Morrison on November 1, 1986.

RACE IMPLICATIONS

I was quite surprised that the trial jury convicted Mr. McMillian on the testimony presented by the State. The testimony of over a half-dozen black witnesses who testified that Mr. McMillian was at home working on his truck was simply ignored. The testimony of Ralph Myers, who is white, was apparently given more credibility despite the fact that Myers had a lengthy criminal record, his testimony was implausible and despite the many incentives Myers had for lying to help himself.

Race clearly played a role in jury selection and review of the evidence. While the crime took place in Monroe County which has an African-American population of over 40 percent, venue was changed to Baldwin County, Alabama, which has a black population of less than 15 percent. Only one African-American served on Mr. McMillian's jury after the State excluded other black potential jurors through peremptory strikes. The district attorney also improperly told the jury that Mr. McMillian was rumored to have had an affair with a young white woman. The introduction of this evidence had no purpose or relation to this case other than inflaming racial prejudice against Mr. McMillian.

Despite the extremely weak and contradictory evidence against Mr. McMillian, the Alabama Court of Criminal Appeals concluded on appeal that there was sufficient evidence to affirm Mr. McMillian's conviction and death sentence. Even after evidence was presented that established that witnesses testifying against Mr. McMillian had received reward money and other favors from the State, Mr. McMillian's conviction and death sentence were affirmed by the Alabama Court of Criminal Appeals.

EVIDENCE OF INNOCENCE

Throughout my representation of Mr. McMillian we continued to investigate his case, and we constantly found evidence to support his innocence. We were able to confirm that Mr. McMillian's truck was not a low-rider in November of 1986; we gathered evidence which showed that Ralph Myers did not even know who Mr. McMillian was in March of 1987, some four months after he allegedly committed this crime; we discovered that the State arranged for Bill Hooks to be removed from jail so that he could inspect Mr. McMillian's truck before Hooks gave a written statement stating he saw Mr. McMillian's truck at the crime scene; we also found evidence which proved that law enforcement officials knowingly concealed information which would have helped establish Mr. McMillian's innocence prior to trial.

In August of 1991, we were contacted by the State's witness Ralph Myers. Mr. Myers told us that his trial testimony against Mr. McMillian was false. Mr. Myers told us that he was pressured by law enforcement officers to testify falsely against Mr. McMillian. Mr. Myers' admission that he testified falsely against Mr. McMillian opened up additional avenues of investigation that also produced evidence of law enforcement misconduct and abuse.

We also uncovered other statements Myers made directly to law enforcement officials where Myers made it clear that he had no knowledge of Mr. McMillian's involvement in this offense and that any assertion to the contrary would be a lie. These statements, made even before Mr. McMillian's arrest, were concealed from the defense and the jury.

In May of 1992, we presented all of the evidence we uncovered before a Circuit Court judge in Baldwin County, Alabama, including testimony from Ralph Myers who admitted that his trial testimony was false. Despite all of this evidence, the court ruled against us and held that Mr. McMillian was not entitled to relief or a new trial. It was the fifth time since Mr. McMillian's capital murder conviction and death sentence had been imposed in 1988 that an Alabama State court had refused to grant Mr. McMillian relief or a new trial after legal challenges of newly discovered evidence had been presented.

It took an additional nine months of litigation before we finally convinced the Alabama Court of Criminal Appeals to overturn Mr.

McMillian's capital murder conviction and sentence of death. During the year and a half following Myers' admission that his testimony was false and the discovery of the State's unlawful concealment of exculpatory evidence the State vigorously opposed our efforts to achieve Mr. McMillian's release. Even after the State's only other witnesses, Bill Hooks and Joe Hightower, both admitted to State investigators in December of 1992 that their trial testimony against McMillian was false, the State still refused to acknowledge Mr. McMillian's innocence. At no point prior to the reversal of Mr. McMillian's capital murder conviction did the State concede that Mr. McMillian's rights had been violated or that he was entitled to relief.

It was only after we filed a motion to dismiss all charges on March 2, 1993, that the State finally acknowledged Mr. McMillian's innocence and joined us in seeking dismissal of the charges against him. The ease with which Mr. McMillian was convicted of capital murder and sentenced to death for a crime he did not commit, contrasted with the enormous difficulties we encountered in establishing his innocence and achieving his release, say much about the criminal justice system and innocence and the death penalty. That it took four and a half years of litigation with thousands of hours of investigation to free Mr. McMillian after wrongfully convicting him in two days shows us that there are disturbing problems which must be corrected within our criminal justice system.

READING

11

STATE COURT AND CAPITAL DEFENDANTS: THE COUNTERPOINT

Kenneth S. Nunnelley

Kenneth S. Nunnelley gave the following statement in his capacity as Deputy Attorney General, Capital Litigation Division, of the State of Alabama Office of the Attorney General.

■ **POINTS TO CONSIDER**

1. How does the author characterize the actions of the State of Alabama in the Walter McMillian case? Contrast this with the portrayal of the State in the previous reading.

2. Discuss the author's contention that the Walter McMillian case represents a success, rather than a failure, of the criminal justice system in Alabama.

3. Summarize the various ways in which the states are better prepared than the federal courts to handle claims of innocence, according to the author.

Excerpted from the testimony of Kenneth S. Nunnelley before the House of Representatives Committee on the Judiciary, July 23, 1993.

What occurred in the McMillian case proves that the states are well equipped to deal with newly discovered evidence claims in capital cases.

Walter McMillian was released from the Alabama Prison System after evidence developed by the State established that McMillian had been wrongly convicted of capital murder and sentenced to death. However, as unfortunate as that situation is, it does not indicate that the criminal justice system somehow failed Mr. McMillian. Instead, what occurred in the McMillian case proves that the states are well equipped to deal with newly discovered evidence claims in capital cases.

SUCCESS OF THE SYSTEM

McMillian's conviction and death sentence were reversed by the Alabama Court of Criminal Appeals, the first appellate court to hear his case. That fact alone demonstrates that the state courts are well able to protect the rights of capital defendants.

The Alabama Court of Criminal Appeals reversed McMillian's conviction and sentence regarding a finding of a violation of Brady v. Maryland, based upon perjured testimony. Most importantly, the evidence that was withheld in violation of Brady was not evidence that suggested that someone other than McMillian committed this murder, but was evidence that could have been used on cross-examination of Ralph Myers who was McMillian's cohort.

While the Court of Criminal Appeals did not disturb the finding of the trial court that Myers did not commit perjury at McMillian's trial, it is virtually certain that he did. Myers was a suspect in an unrelated capital murder in a neighboring county, and it is clear that Myers' false testimony against McMillian was the final act in a scheme developed by Myers to avoid the death penalty for another murder. What is also clear is the loathsome nature of the perjury committed by Myers, Hooks and Hightower. However, the testimony of these three witnesses, who were the key witnesses against McMillian, withstood extensive cross-examination by McMillian's trial lawyer, J.D. Chestnutt. Mr. Chestnutt, who is black, is one of the most respected criminal defense lawyers in Alabama. Moreover, Hooks' perjury was not revealed during extensive cross-examination by McMillian's lawyer. Hooks, who is also black, did not admit to having perjured himself until earli-

© **Tribune Media Services**, Inc. Reprinted with permission.

er. That admission was made during the course of a joint investigation conducted by the Attorney General's Office and the Alabama Bureau of Investigation which was initiated following Myers' admission of perjury. Hightower's perjury was also discovered during that investigation.

There is little doubt that Hooks' motivation to commit perjury was the hope of receiving some reward. He admitted as much, and, during his last interview with state investigators, asked if his admission of perjury meant that he had to return the reward. On the other hand, Hightower's perjury seems to have been an attempt to gain favor with local law enforcement authorities. However, the indisputable fact, and the one that is most pertinent here, is the fact that the State went to great lengths to investigate the allegation of perjury and, when that allegation proved to be true, immediately informed the Court of Criminal Appeals and McMillian's attorney and dismissed the indictment against McMillian. There is not one shred of evidence to suggest that the State had anything at all to do with the perjury that occurred in this case. That disgusting series of events was the product of Myers, Hooks and Hightower, no one else.

MCMILLIAN, STATE COURTS AND CLAIMS OF INNOCENCE

McMillian's conviction and sentence, however, were reversed at the first stage of direct review and therefore never reached the State post-conviction or federal *habeas corpus* stage. Newly discovered evidence claims can be raised at any time in an Alabama state post-conviction proceeding so long as the claim is raised within six months of the discovery of the new evidence. Moreover, even if McMillian had not raised the claim upon which the Court of Criminal Appeals reversed his conviction and sentence until the federal *habeas* stage, that claim would not have been procedurally barred and the federal courts would have reached the merits of the claim. Finally, the facts present in the McMillian case would not have failed to produce executive clemency, even if the claim had not been raised in any judicial proceeding.

STATES ARE WELL-EQUIPPED

The states are well able to deal with claims of newly discovered evidence, as the McMillian case indicates. Two other examples of death-sentenced inmates who received relief from the state courts in cases involving claims of innocence are Randall Dale Adams and Clarence Brantley, both of whom were under death sentences in Texas.

In addition to those inmates, recent events establish that governors of states having capital punishment take their clemency power seriously, and will not allow an execution to be carried out if any doubt remains. For example, Anson Maynard received executive clemency in North Carolina because the governor "just was not sure." Governor Wilder of Virginia recently granted clemency to Joseph M. Giarratano and Herbert R. Bassette for similar reasons. In the Roger Coleman case, which also arose from Virginia, Governor Wilder went to great lengths to determine the true facts of that case, in spite of massive media coverage which proclaimed Coleman's innocence. In fact, Governor Wilder had a polygraph examination given before making the decision to deny clemency. The media coverage that accompanied that case has since been proven to be little more than hype and a civil lawsuit is now pending on behalf of the individual whom Coleman's attorneys claimed was the true perpetrator. The

HERRERA V. COLLINS

Much has been made of a misinterpretation of the Herrera decision to the effect that the decision would allow the states to execute a defendant for a crime that he did not commit. Justice O'Connor's concurring opinion makes clear that Herrera does not stand for that proposition. Justice O'Connor stated, "I cannot disagree with the fundamental legal principle that executing the innocent is inconsistent with the Constitution" and "the execution of a legally and factually innocent person would be a constitutionally intolerable event." Herrera v. Collins, 113 S.Ct. 853, 870 (1993). As Justice O'Connor stated, the Court assumed for the sake of argument "that a truly persuasive demonstration of actual innocence would render any such execution unconstitutional and that federal *habeas* relief would be warranted if no state avenue were open to process the claim." Id., at 874. That is the holding in Herrera, and any claim to the contrary is simply not correct.

Moreover, Herrera's claim of innocence was weak at best, seeking to blame his dead brother for the crimes Herrera was found guilty of committing. When the evidence against Herrera is considered against the proffered evidence of innocence, it is not surprising that none of the federal judges to hear this claim, including the dissenters in the Supreme Court, have ever expressed any doubt as to Herrera's guilt.

Kenneth S. Nunnelley in Congressional testimony, July 23, 1993.

Coleman case stands as an example of how seriously the governors of capital punishment states view their role.

There is nothing to suggest that the state courts are incapable of protecting the constitutional rights of criminal defendants. In fact, some would argue that the state courts are far more liberal and lenient on constitutional issues than are the federal courts. However, be that as it may, nothing even remotely suggests that the appellate courts of each of the states that have capital punishment are incapable of doing what must be done in protecting the constitutional rights of the criminal defendants whose cases are argued before them.

GRAVITY OF MISTAKEN EXECUTION

My remarks should not in any way be construed as advocating the execution of an innocent person. Nothing could be further from the truth. I have been involved in seven executions in the state of Alabama, and have been counsel in two of those proceedings. There is no more sobering task that a prosecutor can undertake, and I know that my counterparts in all of the capital punishment states feel as serious about their responsibilities as I do. No one involved in capital litigation has any interest whatsoever in seeing the wrong person executed, and I am convinced that no prosecutor would allow that to happen.

READING

12

HABEAS CORPUS REFORM IS NEEDED

Daniel E. Lungren

As Attorney General for the State of California, Daniel E. Lungren testified before the Senate Judiciary Committee in support of controversial reforms in the Writ of Habeas Corpus. A package of Habeas Corpus reforms were passed by Congress and signed into law by President Bill Clinton as part of the 1996 Counter-terrorism legislation.

■ POINTS TO CONSIDER

1. Why does the author see the need for *habeas corpus* reform?

2. Discuss the issue of indigent defense in post-conviction appeals. What are the author's feelings concerning the issue?

3. What is the conflict between the state courts and federal courts?

4. How might *habeas corpus* reform solve this?

Excerpted from the testimony of Dan E. Lungren before the United States Senate Judiciary Committee, March 28, 1995.

Those who have been victimized by crime have a right to expect timely justice. In their case, "justice delayed" is truly "justice denied."

Those of us responsible for handling *habeas corpus* cases have great hope and anticipation that Congress will pass meaningful *habeas corpus* reform. We desire legislation which embodies a concept of justice that is primarily defined by the guilt or innocence of those who claim constitutional violations, rather than dexterity at procedural gamesmanship. The assertion of constitutional violations at the later stages of the process must not be at the expense of the truth-finding function of the criminal justice system. If the guilt or innocence determination of the state courts is to have any meaning at all, there must be some conclusion with respect to the timing and the nature of the claims that may be brought under federal review. In this regard, I would like to support an important step in this direction which was the introduction of the Habeas Corpus Reform Act of 1995.

HISTORIC TIME

We have before us a historic opportunity to enact meaningful reform of the criminal justice system. The American people have spoken in a resounding manner, and we have a solemn responsibility to respond to their concerns. Certainly one important aspect of that message is that "Washington may not always know best," and that the federal government should at a minimum not undermine the ability of states and localities to perform their essential functions. This has particular relevance with respect to the operation of state criminal justices systems.

As the Attorney General of California, I would like to focus my comments on the federal *habeas* interference with appropriate criminal sanctions in the states. I would like to emphasize at the outset that my comments are not meant to be a blanket criticism of the men and women who serve on our federal judiciary. Rather, the source of our difficulty rests with the inadequacy of existing statutory law. This defective nature of the law is particularly pronounced with respect to capital cases where state prisoners have no incentive to resolve their legal claims in a timely fashion.

Because federal *habeas corpus* review of state criminal judgments is a statutory remedy, only Congress can fully reform the system. In this regard, reform of *habeas corpus* procedures does not in any way implicate the "Great Writ" in the U.S. Constitution. In fact a statutory right to federal *habeas corpus* relief for state prisoners did not come into existence until the enactment of of the Habeas Corpus Act of 1867.

It is therefore our task to address the need for reform. In this regard I would like to share with you some of my thoughts concerning the basic elements necessary for meaningful legislation.

The problems relating to abuse of federal *habeas corpus* review are present in a broad class of cases. There are however different incentives with respect to non-capital and capital cases. Under circumstances where a sentence is being served, the petitioner has little reason to prolong the process. However, in a death penalty case, delay becomes a principle objective of the litigation.

STATUTE OF LIMITATIONS

One essential ingredient of general *habeas* reform should be the imposition of a statute of limitations on the filing of state prisoner petitions in federal court. Under the Habeas Corpus Reform Act a one year time limit in the bill would run from the time at which the state judgment is final. Further delay in filing a petition would be limited to those instances where cause is shown. This is a clear improvement over current law which contains no such limitation.

97

EXHAUSTION

The requirement that state prisoners must first exhaust state remedies before seeking federal *habeas* relief has long been a cardinal principle of American law. The United States Supreme Court expressed the doctrine well in Darr v. Burford:

> Because it would be unseemly in our dual system of government for a Federal district court to upset a State court conviction without an opportunity to the State courts to correct a constitutional violation, Federal courts apply the doctrine of comity, which teaches that one court should defer action on causes properly within its jurisdiction until the courts of another sovereignty with concurrent powers and already cognizant of the litigation have had an opportunity to pass upon the matter.

The states have primary responsibility for the enforcement of criminal law. Comity within our judicial system recognizes that state courts are also competent to deal with federal questions by requiring that before the federal courts are to consider the merits of *habeas* claims, the state courts should first be afforded the opportunity to resolve the case, including any legal and factual issues relating to the claim.

AN EFFECTIVE DEATH PENALTY

The abuse of federal *habeas* has had a profound effect on the enforcement of the death penalty in the states. Not a single execution took place in California between 1965 and 1992. California's death row population has now swelled to 400 inmates and only two executions have occurred since 1992.

The number of capital cases pending on federal *habeas corpus* has more than doubled. As of today, the California Supreme Court has affirmed 161 capital judgments. There are now 125 cases before the U.S. District Court on *habeas corpus* review, and four cases pending in the 9th Circuit.

It is perhaps most disturbing that in 1994 there were only two district court decisions which fully disposed of a capital *habeas* petition. Although there were several evidentiary hearings in other capital cases last year, there were no other decisions.

I might also note that as dramatic as these figures are they do not reflect the full costs of the present system. The credibility of the criminal justice system itself is undermined by a maze of procedures which indefinitely prolong the certainty of punishment.

Most significantly, those who have been victimized by crime have a right to expect timely justice. In their case, "justice delayed" is truly "justice denied." Tragically, they find themselves victimized both by the perpetrator of the crime and then again by the system itself. Endless judicial wrangling prolongs their personal agony and makes closure of their grief difficult if not impossible.

POST-CONVICTION COUNSEL

An element inherent in all federal mandates is the misbegotten perspective that Washington is somehow the repository of a superior brand of wisdom. This attitude lacks an appropriate level of respect for state criminal justice systems and is destructive of the comity that is necessary if we are to have any hope of advancing the principle of greater finality.

The appointment of counsel at the primary stages of litigation – at trial and on direct appeal – is already required by the Constitution, and convictions and sentences are subject to reversal if counsel is found to be ineffective at these stages. Our experience shows that qualified counsel are regularly appointed in capital cases in California and any effort to impose requirements on us beyond those required by the Constitution would unnecessarily interfere with existing state protocol and likely reduce the pool of available counsel.

THE HABEAS CORPUS REFORM ACT

The Habeas Corpus Reform Act imposes a statute of limitations for the filing of claims, as well as limitations on the types of claims which can be brought in the latest stages of the *habeas* process. *Habeas corpus* reform should limit review of successive petitions to those concerning the prisoners underlying guilt or innocence. It should be remembered that the essential element of the Powell Committee recommendations was to reject consideration of challenges to the sentencing phase of a capital case on second or successive petitions. This is an integral aspect of reform. As Judge Friendly argued over two decades ago:

A requirement that the prisoner come forward with a showing of innocence identifies those *habeas* petitioners who are justified in again seeking relief from their incarceration.

FEDERAL COURT STANDARD OF REVIEW

An important policy question which should be considered by the Congress involves the level of deference that will be accorded to state judicial systems. In other words, what review should be available on federal *habeas corpus* following the state trial, appeal, and collateral proceedings, and review by the United States Supreme Court?

It must be understood that one of the real costs of *habeas corpus* review is lack of finality. Absent finality, the criminal law loses much of its deterrent effect. As the court in McCleskey v. Zant noted, finality has particular importance in a federal system.

In McCleskey, the court recognized that what is at stake in federal *habeas* proceeding is the enforcement of state criminal laws within state forums. Moreover, in our system of government, state courts are co-equal institutions with their federal counterparts and have the same responsibility to uphold the U.S. Constitution. To permit federal intrusion and independent relitigation of matters properly and reasonably litigated in state court is to relegate state courts to mere fact finding panels whose decisions are ultimately subject to resolution by the federal judiciary.

Federal courts are not superior to state courts merely because the *habeas corpus* statute affords them the last word in the litigation chain. The state courts should not be viewed as a tryout on the road for what will be the determinative federal *habeas* hearing. The question comes to mind whether Judge Malcom Lucas became any less wise or any less committed to the U.S. Constitution when he traded in his federal judicial robe in order to put the one on he now wears as a Justice on the California Supreme Court. Conversely, was former state appellate court judge Sandra Day O'Connor blessed with new wisdom when she assumed her place on the U.S. Supreme Court?

While the federal government may have an interest in the uniform application of constitutional law, that objective is achieved primarily through direct review to the U.S. Supreme Court, and it certainly does not require a review of every aspect of state court decisions via the writ of *habeas corpus.*

Inquiry by the federal courts should focus on the reasonableness of state court decisions. This method of analysis is already performed in the non-retroactivity context of Teague v. Lane where federal courts must resolve whether the legal holdings of state court are "reasonable" in order to determine whether a ruling will be applied retroactively.

The critical point is that a standard of deference which upholds reasonable state court determinations should be a central element of *habeas* reform legislation. In my view this approach would accord an appropriate level of deference to state procedures while at the same time provide the federal courts with the authority to review the question of whether state court adjudications are in fact reasonable. This is essential if we are to realize finality as one of the principal objectives of the law and to make the trial on the merits of the "main event."

13

HABEAS CORPUS MUST NOT BE RESTRICTED

Nicholas deB. Katzenbach

Nicholas deB. Katzenbach was formerly the Attorney General during the Johnson Administration. Katzenbach was one of four former Attorneys General who served as chair of the Emergency Committee to Save Habeas Corpus.

■ POINTS TO CONSIDER

1. Summarize the purpose and history of the "Great Writ," according to the author.

2. Discuss the problems with federalism and *habeas corpus* review as Katzenbach describes.

3. According to the reading, what is the problem with deference to the states as part of *habeas corpus* reform?

4. Why does the author describe "one bite at the apple" as "no bite at the apple?"

5. Summarize the importance of post-conviction counsel for indigents.

Excerpted from the testimony of Nicholas deB. Katzenbach before the Senate Judiciary Committee, March 28, 1995.

No person should pay with his life for the neglect or ignorance of his lawyer.

First, *habeas corpus* is the means by which we hold government – state or federal – accountable for Due Process in criminal matters. It is the Great Writ, the fundamental underpinning of all our freedoms, perhaps our greatest heritage. I begin with this reminder because tinkering with something so fundamental requires both legislative wisdom and, if I may, a little legislative humility as well.

PROBLEMS WITH FEDERALISM

Second, undoubtedly the writ does raise problems of federalism, and efforts to avoid unnecessary intrusion into state responsibilities are understandable. But those problems, at bottom, stem from the fourteenth amendment and its requirement that states adhere to the standards of the Federal Constitution.

Third, problems of federalism come from post-conviction review in federal courts of state convictions, particularly in capital cases. Whatever tensions this review creates could be greatly reduced, and money saved, by the simple expedient of ensuring competent counsel at trial. Indeed, this simple requirement would probably accomplish more at less cost than the rest of the proposed procedural reforms put together.

Finally, it does not seem to me either wise or prudent to legislate cutbacks on rules and practices designed as safeguards against execution of the innocent. There is an unacceptably high level of complexity in the current law. There are *habeas* proceedings that drag on far longer than they ought to, and the process should be streamlined. We believe, however, that this mission can be accomplished without curtailing the federal courts' ability to enforce the Bill of Rights.

The federal courts have no higher mission than to uphold the Constitution, and *habeas corpus* has been, since the founding of the Republic, the primary means of access to the federal courts for people unconstitutionally imprisoned. It is the only opportunity most state prisoners have to get an independent review of their federal constitutional claims. It places enforcement of the Bill of Rights in the hands of life-tenured federal judges, as a check on state judges who must often stand for election and face powerful pressures to produce swift and popular results. Throughout history, it has been the last bulwark against injustices born of racial prejudice and intolerance. It has saved the innocent from imprisonment or execution.

And most importantly, in keeping open a meaningful remedy for unconstitutional detentions, it safeguards the rights of all Americans. More than a century ago, Chief Justice Salmon Chase wrote that *habeas corpus* "has been for centuries esteemed the best and only sufficient defense of personal freedom." *Ex Parte Yeager*, 75 U.S. 85, 95 (1868).

An example of the vital role of *habeas corpus* was the case of an indigent state prisoner in Florida named Clarence Earl Gideon. Some 30 years ago, after reviewing his handwritten *habeas corpus* petition, the U.S. Supreme Court granted him a new trial because the state had prosecuted him without providing him with counsel in violation of the Sixth Amendment. The Court held that in all future felony prosecutions throughout the land, the Bill of Rights would require states to provide counsel to indigent defendants.

Habeas corpus is the basis of all our freedoms. Tinkering with it is always a dangerous proposition, and must be done very carefully – more carefully, perhaps, than amending the Constitution itself, for it is *habeas corpus* that gives life to all of the Constitution's various guarantees of individual liberty. It is *habeas corpus* which embodies the entire notion of individual rights against the government – a tradition rooted in the Magna Carta and enshrined in the Constitution.

THE LEGISLATION

The destructive impact of a deference requirement on the power of the federal courts to enforce the United States Constitution can hardly be overstated. Whichever formulation is considered, the danger remains the same: that federal courts will be unconditionally barred from assessing the constitutionality of certain state judgments – judgments involving the most awesome power of the states over their citizens, the power to strip them of their liberty or life. However wide this band of mandated deference may turn out to be, there will in every state be some body of case law interpreting the U.S. Constitution which may be clearly wrong, but not so unreasonably wrong as to permit the federal courts to correct the error. Where this line lies, between unconstitutional results

Cartoon by Bill Sanders. Reprinted with permission.

and unreasonably unconstitutional results, will unquestionably provide full-time work for legions of lawyers and judges for a great many years, and breed precisely the type of confusion and delay that this legislation was designed to eliminate.

Under this regime, the fifty states would be free to develop their own wrong – but not too wrong – interpretations of what the Federal Constitution means, and the federal courts would be powerless to intervene to restore uniform nationwide constitutional protections. The Constitution could protect against racially motivated practices or police abuse less in one state than in another. The Bill of Rights could mean different things in different states. The dangers of this have been recognized since the founding of the Republic: the first Chief Justice, John Marshall, warned in 1821 that if state court rulings on federal issues could not be reviewed by federal courts, the result would be "a hydra in government from which nothing but contradiction and confusion can spread." Cohens v. Virginia, 19 U.S. 264, 414. And as Rep.

Robert Scott commented during House Judiciary deliberations, we are all fortunate that the federal courts were not required to defer to the states when Brown v. Board of Education came along.

Actually, there seems to be some confusion about what the various reform proposals mean – how much deference, if any, Congress intends to require the federal courts to give the states on federal constitutional questions. Proponents of the most restrictive reform legislation commonly criticize the numerous trips through federal review currently allowed, and sound the theme of restricting federal *habeas corpus* to "one bite at the apple." Members of Congress less intimately involved with the *habeas* debate may be forgiven for assuming that the "full and fair" language describes the type of review that will be available during that one trip through the Federal System, as opposed to preventing any federal review at all. Chairman Hatch described "full and fair" in the last Congress as allowing petitioners to "go through the federal process one time, and that is it. If their claim was 'fully and fairly litigated,' that is it." *Cong. Rec.*, Nov. 16, 1993, at S15744. And Attorney General William Barr, even while proposing a "full and fair" deference requirement, muddied the waters by explaining that the goal was to allow "one full course of litigation through the state courts and federal *habeas corpus* proceedings" (letter to Speaker of the House, September 10, 1990).

NO BITE AT THE APPLE

It is important to understand that "full and fair" and the other deference requirements represent the polar opposite of "one bite." They represent "no bite." They stand for the theory that the very existence of federal review of state judgments is offensive to the states, impugning their competence, and is unnecessary and duplicative. Perhaps the leading proponent of "full and fair," former Congressman and current California Attorney General Dan Lungren, sees the "relitigation" of claims already litigated in state court as leading to the "denigration of comity" and causing "undue friction" with the states (testimony before House Judiciary Committee, June 27, 1991).

We must expect states, and state attorneys general, to take offense at federal *habeas corpus*. Every *habeas* petition granted is essentially a constitutional rebuke to them. Their desire for less federal oversight and more "comity" is natural and understandable.

FALSE REFORM

The supporters of so-called *habeas* reform usually do not tell us other stories – the rest of the story. They do not tell us about innocent defendants sent to death row because they could not afford competent counsel, and because some states do not have procedures in place to provide effective counsel to indigents. They do not tell us of murder defendants watching as their attorneys fail to properly prepare and present a defense, either because they lack resources or because they themselves are indifferent, incompetent, or inexperienced. They do not tell us about innocent defendants convicted because of sloppy investigations or prosecutorial misconduct.

Excerpted from the statement of Senator Russell Feingold (D-WI) on the floor of the Senate, June 7, 1995.

But their taking offense does not end the matter. Constitutional violations sometimes occur in the states, and are sometimes not corrected through state processes. The provisions of the Constitution are binding on the states through the fourteenth amendment, and no statutory directive for federal court deference can change that. Nothing short of cutting back the fourteenth amendment itself can relieve the states of their obligation to follow the Constitution, or the federal courts of their obligation to enforce it.

The fact is that, the states' taking umbrage notwithstanding, federal *habeas corpus* review remains an important and all too frequently necessary check on the constitutionality of state actions. Our fundamental message today is: trimming *habeas corpus* procedures is a legitimate and worthwhile goal. Trimming the substantive scope of the federal courts' ability to protect constitutional freedoms is not. It is unwise, unnecessary and potentially unconstitutional.

Often capital cases involving indigent defendants – (which is virtually the only kind of capital defendant) – are assigned to lawyers who are inexperienced or given severely inadequate resources to investigate the case or prepare a defense. Factual and legal issues which are undeveloped or improperly preserved can never be reopened on *habeas corpus*. Witnesses who were not interviewed, an alibi that was not thought worth investigating, evidence of mental retardation that was never developed for lack of money for a psychiatrist, evidence of government misconduct in coercing a confession or suppressing exculpatory evidence – all are barred if not correctly preserved at trial.

In the Coleman v. Thompson case in 1991, a death row inmate with strong new evidence of actual innocence – evidence so powerful and disturbing that *Time* magazine featured it as a cover story – was denied an opportunity to even have his new evidence heard in federal court, because his lawyer had unwittingly missed a filing deadline by three days. The Court ruled that the mistake of the otherwise competent lawyer, who was with the respected Washington firm of Arnold & Porter, barred any *habeas* review of the evidence. Mr. Coleman was executed.

Such rulings devalue the protections of the Bill of Rights. No person should pay with his life for the neglect or ignorance of his lawyer.

COMPETENT COUNSEL

It is essential that indigent defendants on trial for their lives be represented by competent and adequately paid counsel appointed by an independent body responsible for maintaining a list of qualified lawyers. Consistent with notions of federalism, states could be allowed to provide a lesser level of counsel if they wish, but the federal courts should not then be required to sort through the various procedural doctrines which presume that the state court trial was full and correct, and should simply proceed directly to the merits of the *habeas* claim.

We also urge attention to the innocence portions of the pending proposals. Each of the current bills would apparently overrule the recent Supreme Court case of Schlup v. Delo, 115 S.Ct. 851 (1995) by setting a higher burden of proof for newly discovered evidence of actual innocence. For the minute number of cases where the evidence shows a probability that the petitioner is completely innocent, it is unimaginable that there could be any objection to permitting the filing of a petition at any time before the execution is carried out. In fact, we assume that the overruling of Schlup is not intended, since the leading bills such as S. 3 were drafted before the case was handed down.

Vast improvements in speed and finality can be obtained without encroaching on constitutional protections or sacrificing the life or liberty of an innocent person.

POVERTY AND THE DEATH PENALTY: WHAT IS EDITORIAL BIAS?

This activity may be used as an individualized study guide for students in libraries and resource centers or as a discussion catalyst in small group and classroom discussions.

The capacity to recognize an author's point of view is an essential reading skill. The skill to read with insight and understanding involves the ability to detect different kinds of opinions or bias. **Sex bias, race bias, ethnocentric bias, political bias** and **religious bias** are five basic kinds of opinions expressed in editorials and all literature that attempts to persuade. They are briefly defined in the glossary below.

Glossary of Terms for Reading Skills

Sex Bias – the expression of dislike for and/or feeling of superiority over the opposite sex or a particular sexual minority

Race Bias – the expression of dislike for and/or feeling of superiority over a racial group

Ethnocentric Bias – the expression of a belief that one's own group, race, religion, culture or nation is superior. Ethnocentric persons judge others by their own standards and values.

Political Bias – the expression of political opinions and attitudes about domestic or foreign affairs

Religious Bias – the expression of a religious belief or attitude

---

Guidelines

1. From the readings in Chapter Three, locate five sentences that provide examples of **editorial opinion** or **bias**.

2. Write down each of the above sentences and determine what kind of bias each sentence represents. Is it **sex bias, race bias, ethnocentric bias, political bias** or **religious bias?**

3. Read through the following statements and decide which ones represent a form of **editorial bias**. Evaluate each statement by using the method indicated below:

• **Mark (S)** for any statements that reflect *sex bias*.

• **Mark (R)** for *race bias*.

• **Mark (E)** for *ethnocentric bias*.

• **Mark (P)** for *political bias*.

• **Mark (F)** for statements that are *factual*.

_____ 1. As the population on death row continues to grow, the number of lawyers willing to subject themselves to the expense of representing poor inmates in the final states of their appeals is shrinking.

_____ 2. All those sentenced to death are able to get legal representation at public expense in the final stages of the appeals process.

_____ 3. If two suspects, one poor and one wealthy, are charged with separate capital crimes, the quality of justice is very different.

_____ 4. Race, not wealth, was the most important factor in the O.J. Simpson case.

_____ 5. Most people on death row are distinguished by their abject poverty, mental impairments and minimal intelligence.

_____ 6. One example of the failure of the capital punishment system is the number of mentally retarded people who have been executed.

_____ 7. One example of the success of the capital punishment system is how popular it is with the general public.

_____ 8. Mentally retarded defendants don't have the same degree of moral culpability as other members of society.

_____ 9. People in abject poverty do not have the same degree of moral culpability as other members of society.

_____ 10. Since poor people commit more crimes, it is only logical that more poor people will be sentenced to die for capital crimes.

_____ 11. Inadequate legal representation does not occur in just a few capital cases; it is pervasive in the death belt states of the south.

_____ 12. Public defenders in the death belt states are burdened with oppressive caseloads two to five times higher than the national standards.

CHAPTER 4

THE DEATH PENALTY AND THE DISADVANTAGED

READING

14

THE RETARDED, TOO, MUST PAY FOR THEIR CRIMES

Mona Charen

Mona Charen is a prominent conservative commentator. Her column is syndicated nationally.

■ **POINTS TO CONSIDER**

1. According to Charen, how does Penry demonstrate an understanding of his actions despite his attorneys' declarations of his incapability of understanding the nature of his acts?

2. For the author, why can the criminal justice system not "excuse" violent criminals because of severe mitigating factors?

3. In the Supreme Court decision of Penry v. Lynaugh (1989), why did the majority on the Court agree with Charen that Mr. Penry should be executed despite mental retardation?

Charen, Mona, "Should Retarded Criminals Be Executed?" **Conservative Chronicle**, 18 Jan. 1989, p. 28. By permission of Mona Charen and Creators Syndicate.

But while one cannot help but feel pity for the criminal...to excuse his crimes would be a step down the road to forgiving all crimes.

They say that John Paul Penry, a rapist and murderer, has a mental age of seven. His lawyers tell the Supreme Court justices that they must not allow him to die – because he didn't understand the nature of his acts.

A BRUTAL CRIME

Years ago, Penry was out on parole after serving time for rape. While making a delivery, he had seen a 22-year-old mother with long brown hair who appealed to him. On the morning of Oct. 25, 1979, Pamela Mosely Carpenter was at home making Halloween decorations for the Central Baptist Church. Here's how Penry himself described the events of that day in Livingstone, Texas:

"I went over to her house and circled around the block to see if her husband was there. I saw a pickup, so I went to the kitchen door to see if he was there. She came to the door. I asked her if her husband was there and she said 'no.' That's when I jerked the screen door open, pulled my knife out and grabbed her. She was screaming and hollering for help and knocked the knife out of my hand..."

Carpenter then grabbed a scissors and stabbed her attacker twice in the back.

"I banged her hand against the floor and the scissors fell out...She told the dog, which I had not seen, to bite me. I kicked it in the throat and he slid under the bed...While she was on the floor I kicked her two or three times with my foot and stomped her once."

The rape, by Penry's account, went on for half an hour.

When it was over, he explained that he was going to have to kill her, because he was afraid she would "squeal." Raising the scissors over his head, Penry plunged it into her chest. He thought she was dead, but as he moved off she reached for the scissors herself. "This scared me," he said, "and I forget all about getting her money. I ran out the door and boogied."

Pamela Carpenter bled to death before paramedics could reach her.

SOLID UNDERSTANDING

Lawyers for Penry are now claiming that because their client has tested as retarded, he was incapable of forming the requisite intent for the crimes of rape and murder and that executing him would amount to "cruel and unusual punishment." In what sound like carefully scripted responses, Penry now says that he doesn't know whether he committed the crime, but that if he did, he didn't know what he was doing.

It doesn't wash. Penry displayed a perfect grasp of logic when he checked for the husband's car, and a solid understanding of consequences when he killed his victim to prevent her from testifying against him. Moreover, at the time of the crime, a special jury considered the question of whether Penry was competent to stand trial. Another jury rejected his claim of not guilty by reason of mental defect, and the same jury further found that he had acted deliberately.

Clearly, the current law provides abundant opportunities to prove incompetence. Penry flunked out. Joe Price, the district attorney who originally prosecuted the case, thinks Penry's low I.Q. is beside the point. "He's been diagnosed as a sociopath," explains Price, "and that makes him the most cold-blooded killer possible."

VIOLENT PAST, PRESENT

It's true. And Penry has come by his viciousness honestly. As a child, he was burned, beaten and kicked by his mother who kept him locked in a closet for much of his early life and forced him to eat his own feces and drink his own urine. With a childhood like that, how could he not hate the world and particularly women?

But while one cannot help but feel pity for the criminal, and while the mother seems the true villain, our justice system cannot grant ultimate or complete justice. Penry was a victim, but then so perhaps was his mother. To excuse his crimes would be a step down the road to forgiving all crimes. What criminal has not suffered?

In fact, Penry's own horrible suffering makes his punishment all the more necessary – because there is little doubt that given half a chance, he will rape and murder again. The Supreme Court's job

COURT AFFIRMS

Penry's second claim is that it would be cruel and unusual punishment, prohibited by the Eighth Amendment, to execute a mentally retarded person like himself with the reasoning capacity of a seven-year-old. He argues that because of their mental disabilities, mentally retarded people do not possess the level of moral culpability to justify imposing the death sentence. He also argues that there is an emerging national consensus against executing the mentally retarded. The State responds that there is insufficient evidence of a national consensus against executing the retarded, and that existing procedural safeguards adequately protect the interests of mentally retarded persons such as Penry.

Penry does not offer any evidence of the general behavior of juries with respect to sentencing mentally retarded defendants, nor of decisions of prosecutors. He points instead to several public opinion surveys that indicate strong public opposition to execution of the retarded. For example, a poll taken in Texas found that 86% of those polled supported the death penalty, but 73% opposed its application to the mentally retarded.

On the record before the Court today, however, I cannot conclude that all mentally retarded people of Penry's ability – by virtue of their mental retardation alone, and apart from any individualized consideration of their personal responsibility – inevitably lack the cognitive, volitional, and moral capacity to act with the degree of culpability associated with the death penalty. Mentally retarded persons are individuals whose abilities and experiences can vary greatly.

Mental retardation is a factor that may well lessen a defendant's culpability for a capital offense. But we cannot conclude today that the Eighth Amendment precludes the execution of any mentally retarded person of Penry's ability convicted of a capital offense simply by virtue of his or her mental retardation alone. So long as sentencers can consider and give effect to mitigating evidence of mental retardation in imposing sentence, an individualized determination whether "death is the appropriate punishment" can be made in each particular case. While a national consensus against execution of the mentally retarded may someday emerge reflecting the "evolving standards of decency that mark the progress of a maturing society," there is insufficient evidence of such a consensus today.

Excerpted from the majority opinion of the United States Supreme Court in Penry v. Lynaugh (1989), authored by Justice Sandra Day O'Connor, 492 US 302, 106 L Ed 2d 256, 190 S Ct 2934.

is easy. They must decide only whether John Paul Penry should receive earthly punishment. The difficult job of ultimate justice belongs to God.

READING

15

EXECUTING THE RETARDED IS AN AFFRONT TO MORALITY

Robert F. Drinan

Robert F. Drinan, S.J. is a Catholic priest and a prominent national religious spokesman for peace and justice issues. He is a regular contributor to the National Catholic Reporter, *a journal of religion and politics. He wrote the following article for the* Christian Century.

■ **POINTS TO CONSIDER**

1. Why does the execution of the retarded demonstrate the "freakishness" of capital punishment for Drinan and other opponents?

2. Discuss why executing the retarded conflicts with the idea of retribution, according to the article.

3. Summarize what Drinan reports as American religious and lay standards on executing the retarded.

The execution of retarded persons conflicts with the idea of retribution. Retribution cannot be achieved if the person punished does not understand what he did.

Johnny Paul Penry, who has an IQ between 50 and 63, a mental age of six or seven and the social maturity of a child between the ages of eight and ten. Penry also happens to be an admitted killer awaiting execution in Texas, whose case was argued before the U.S. Supreme Court on January 11, 1989.

Penry's crime is without doubt horrendous. On the morning of October 25, 1979, while delivering a refrigerator to Pamela Moseley Carpenter's home in Livingstone, Texas, Penry, then 22, beat and raped her. He then fatally stabbed her with a pair of scissors which Carpenter, 21, was using to make Halloween decorations. In the hours before she died, Carpenter gave the police a description of her assailant which led to Penry's arrest and confession.

LIMITED MENTAL ABILITY

At a competency hearing before trial, Penry was shown to have limited mental ability. He could not read or write, never having finished the first grade. His IQ indicated mild to moderate retardation. He had been in and out of a number of state institutions and had been beaten and abused as a child. Nevertheless, a jury found him competent to stand trial.

At Penry's trial three psychiatrists differed as to whether he was insane. But all of them agreed that Penry had mental limitations, caused perhaps by a birth trauma or by factors in his childhood, such as being locked in his room for extended periods. They also agreed that Penry's problems manifested themselves in an inability to learn from mistakes. The jury rejected Penry's insanity defense and found him guilty of capital murder. He was sentenced to death.

Little response to Penry's pleas that he is illiterate and retarded has been forthcoming in his multiple appeals. Though a federal judge in Texas asserted that "examples of Penry's mental deficiency abound" and that blame for his condition "lies at several doorsteps," Carpenter's brother, former Washington Redskins player Mark Moseley, summed up the reaction of many other observers: "You cannot arbitrarily say that because a guy is mentally retarded he is not responsible for his actions. He knew what he was doing was wrong...and he knew enough to know that if she did testify against him, he was in bad shape. So he did away with her."

Eleven organizations have filed briefs in favor of Penry's petition. James W. Ellis, a law professor and the president of the American Association on Mental Retardation, makes this argument:

> Of all the convicted murderers in this country, fewer than two percent are ever sentenced to death, and only a fraction of these are actually executed. The Supreme Court has held that the only constitutional basis for selecting those who can be executed...is the level of their personal responsibility for their crime. No person with mental retardation is in that top one or two percent in his level of understanding, and foresight, and responsibility.

The NAACP, one of the groups supporting Penry, said that of the 105 murderers executed since capital punishment was reinstated in 1976, at least six were diagnosed as mentally retarded, but the issue was raised too late or not at all.

A PUNISHMENT FOR THE INDIGENT

For those of us who are opposed to the death penalty on moral and constitutional grounds, the possibility of executing a mentally retarded person demonstrates the freakishness of the process by which 2,200 have ended up on death row. They constitute a tiny percent of those convicted of murder. Those with little access to resources, such as blacks, illiterates and the retarded, end up receiving the ultimate punishment. A special heinousness attends the execution of those who, as far as we can perceive, are on the margins of rationality and the edge of responsibility.

We are by no means certain of what went on in the mind of Penry when he assaulted Carpenter. It is easy to condemn him and insist that he had to know what he was doing. But we can't assess the rage and the uncontrollable anger that might have driven this abused and humiliated man on the fateful morning when he came on business to Carpenter's home.

If Penry is to be excused from the death penalty because we don't know how irresistible his acts were, does this mean that all murderers are to be similarly excused? Probably. One of the many arguments used by the opponents of the death penalty is that we know relatively little about the ultimate reasons why individuals engage in violence. Such conduct has to be punished by incarceration. But what moral norms justify society's sitting in judgment on the violence of others and deciding that some will die for their outbursts, but others will only go to jail?

AUTHENTIC RETRIBUTION

For those who believe in the death penalty, the execution of retarded persons conflicts with the idea of retribution. Retribution cannot be achieved if the person punished does not understand what he did.

Centuries ago Anglo-American law decreed that an insane person should not be punished if it is established that he cannot comprehend the nature of the criminal act with which he is charged. Controversies over how to establish the minimum level of comprehension required for criminality have not displaced this basic assumption. In 1986 the Supreme Court excluded insane persons from the death penalty.

In 1988 the Supreme Court decided that a man who was under 16 when he committed a murder may not be executed. Can a court now decree that 32-year-old man deserves the death penalty, even though he has the mental capacity of a young child?

The Supreme Court may at least by implication attempt to resolve that question, but the court's decision will in all probability be based on narrower grounds. The court may try to fashion a remedy for Penry's case without furnishing a loophole for up to 30 percent of the 2,200 inmates on death row.

EVOLVING STANDARDS OF DECENCY

If the Supreme Court does set aside the death penalty for Penry, its decision will find widespread acceptance. A survey conducted by Amnesty International in Florida shows that 71 percent of the respondents opposed the execution of the mentally retarded. A comparable Texas poll revealed that 73 percent of those answering opposed the execution of the retarded, although 86 percent supported capital punishment. Georgia has passed a law banning

121

execution of the mentally retarded, and the Texas legislature plans to take up the issue soon. Its decision would not be applicable to Penry, but it could precipitate a reprieve.

Chief Justice William Rehnquist, Justice Antonin Scalia and Justice Byron White will in all probability vote to sustain the death penalty for Penry. (In 1988 they refused to excuse a 15-year-old boy.) Justice Anthony Kennedy's attitude is unknown. A majority of the Supreme Court could find – as it did in the case of the 15-year-old – that under the "evolving standards of decency that mark the progress of a maturing society," no state may execute a person who committed a capital offense when he has the intelligence and maturity of an eight-year-old child.

U.S. mainline Protestant and Catholic groups continue to oppose the death penalty, along with most Jewish theologians. The most definitive statement on capital punishment by the U.S. Catholic bishops came in November, 1980. By a vote of 145 to 31 with 14 abstentions, the bishops resolved that the penalty should be done away with as "a manifestation of our belief in the unique worth and dignity of each person from the moment of conception, a creature made in the image and likeness of God."

If the Supreme Court refuses to allow Penry to die, its decision will bring the country and the world a bit closer to the position stated eloquently by Nobel Laureate Andrei Sakharov:

> I regard the death penalty as a savage and immoral institution that undermines the moral and legal foundations of a society. I reject the notion that the death penalty has any essential deterrent effect on potential offenders. I am convinced that the contrary is true – that savagery begets only savagery.

READING

16

EXECUTION OF THE INSANE: THE POINT

Justice Thurgood Marshall

President Kennedy nominated Thurgood Marshall to the Second Circuit Court of Appeals on September 23, 1961.

President Johnson nominated Judge Marshall as Solicitor General of the United States on July 13, 1965. He took the oath of office on August 24, 1965.

He was nominated by President Johnson as Associate Justice of the Supreme Court of the United States on June 13, 1967, confirmed by the Senate on August 30, 1967, and took the constitutional oath on September 1, 1967. He took the judicial oath and was seated on October 2, 1967, as successor to Justice Tom Clark. He was the first black person to become a Justice of the Supreme Court. He retired on October 1, 1991 and died January 24, 1993.

■ POINTS TO CONSIDER

1. How does Justice Marshall rule concerning the constitutionality of the death penalty and the insane? Upon what does he base this ruling?

2. Summarize the concerns Justice Marshall has with the Florida procedures to determine the sanity of Alvin Ford.

3. Discuss the important element in procedures to determine sanity that must be present, according to Justice Marshall, to withstand the Eighth Amendment challenge.

Excerpted from the majority opinion of the United States Supreme Court in **Ford v. Wainright** (1986) 477 US 399, 91 L Ed 2d 335, 106 S Ct 2595.

For today, no less than before, we may seriously question the retributive value of executing a person who has no comprehension of why he has been singled out and stripped of his fundamental right to life.

For centuries no jurisdiction has countenanced the execution of the insane, yet this Court has never decided whether the Constitution forbids the practice. Today we keep faith with our common law heritage in holding that it does.

FORD AND THE STATE

Alvin Bernard Ford was convicted of murder in 1974 and sentenced to death. There is no suggestion that he was incompetent at the time of his offense, at trial, or at sentencing. In early 1982, however, Ford began to manifest gradual changes in behavior. They began as an occasional peculiar idea or confused perception, but became more serious over time.

Counsel for Ford asked a psychiatrist who had examined Ford earlier, Dr. Jamal Amin, to continue seeing him and to recommend appropriate treatment. Dr. Amin concluded in 1983 that Ford suffered from "a severe, uncontrollable, mental disease which closely resembles 'paranoid schizophrenia with suicide potential'" – a "major mental disorder...severe enough to substantially affect Mr. Ford's present ability to assist in the defense of his life."

Counsel for Ford invoked the procedures of Florida law governing the determination of competency of a condemned inmate. Following the procedures set forth in the statute, the Governor of Florida appointed a panel of three psychiatrists to evaluate whether Ford had "the mental capacity to understand the nature of the death penalty and the reasons why it was imposed upon him." At a single meeting, the three psychiatrists together interviewed Ford for approximately 30 minutes. The interview produced three different diagnoses, but accord on the question of sanity as defined by state law.

The Governor's decision was announced on April 30, 1984, when, without explanation or statement, he signed a death warrant for Ford's execution. This Court granted Ford's petition for *certiorari* in order to resolve the important issue whether the Eighth Amendment prohibits the execution of the insane and, if

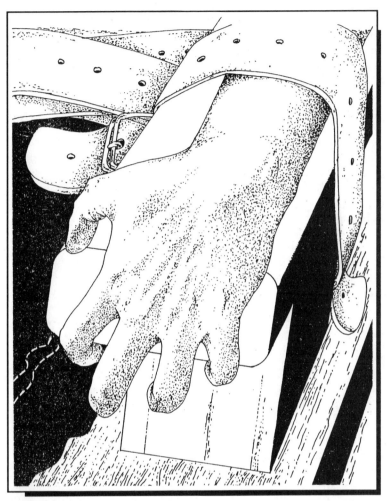

Reprinted with permission from the **Star Tribune**, Minneapolis. Illustration by Craig MacIntosh.

so, whether the District Court should have held a hearing on the petitioner's claim.

EIGHTH AMENDMENT CHALLENGE

Since this Court last had occasion to consider the infliction of the death penalty upon the insane, our interpretations of the Due Process Clause and the Eighth Amendment have evolved substantially. In Solesbee v. Balkom (1950), a condemned prisoner claimed a due process right to a judicial determination of his sanity, yet the Court did not consider the possible existence of a right under the Eighth Amendment, which had not yet been applied to the States. The sole question the Court addressed was whether Georgia's procedure for ascertaining sanity adequately effectuated that State's own policy of sparing the insane from execution.

Now that the Eighth Amendment has been recognized to affect significantly both the procedural and the substantive aspects of the death penalty, the question of executing the insane takes on a wholly different complexion. The adequacy of the procedures chosen by a state to determine sanity, therefore, will depend upon an issue that this Court has never addressed: whether the Constitution places a substantive restriction on the State's power to take the life of an insane prisoner.

We begin, then, with the common law. The bar against executing a prisoner who has lost his sanity bears impressive historical credentials; the practice consistently has been branded "savage and inhuman." 4 W. Blackstone, *Commentaries* *24-*25 (1769).

Further indications suggest that this solid proscription was carried to America, where it was early observed that "the judge is bound" to stay the execution upon insanity of the prisoner. 1 J. Chitty, *A Practical Treatise on the Criminal Law* *761 (5th Am ed 1847).

This ancestral legacy has not outlived its time. Today, no state in the Union permits the execution of the insane. It is clear that the ancient and humane limitation upon the State's ability to execute its sentences has as firm a hold upon the jurisprudence of today as it had centuries ago in England. The various reasons put forth in support of the common law restriction have no less logical, moral, and practical force than they did when first voiced. For today, no less than before, we may seriously question the retributive value of executing a person who has no comprehension of why he has been singled out and stripped of his fundamental right to life. Similarly, the natural abhorrence civilized societies feel at killing one who has no capacity to come to grips with his own conscience or deity is still vivid today. And the intuition that such an execution simply offends humanity is evidently shared across this Nation. Faced with such widespread evidence of a restriction upon sovereign power, this Court is compelled to conclude that the Eighth Amendment prohibits a state from carrying out a sentence of death upon a prisoner who is insane. Whether its aim be to protect the condemned from fear and pain without comfort of understanding, or to protect the dignity of society itself from the barbarity of exacting mindless vengeance, the restriction finds enforcement in the Eighth Amendment.

EXECUTION AND INSANE

The Eighth Amendment prohibits the State from inflicting the penalty of death upon a prisoner who is insane. The petitioner's allegation of insanity in his *habeas corpus* petition, if proved, therefore, would bar his execution. The question before us is whether the District Court was under an obligation to hold an evidentiary hearing on the question of Ford's sanity. In answering that question, we bear in mind that, while the underlying social values encompassed by the Eighth Amendment are rooted in historical traditions, the manner in which our judicial system protects those values is purely a matter of contemporary law. Once a substantive right or restriction is recognized in the Constitution, therefore, its enforcement is in no way confined to the rudimentary process deemed adequate in ages past.

DETERMINATION OF SANITY

Florida law directs the Governor, when informed that a person under sentence of death may be insane, to stay the execution and appoint a commission of three psychiatrists to examine the prisoner.

After submission of the reports of the three examining psychiatrists, reaching conflicting diagnoses but agreeing on the ultimate issue of competency, Ford's counsel attempted to submit to the Governor some other written materials, including the reports of the two other psychiatrists who had examined Ford at greater length, one of whom had concluded that the prisoner was not competent to suffer execution. The Governor's office refused to inform counsel whether the submission would be considered. The Governor subsequently issued his decision in the form of a death warrant. This most cursory form of procedural review fails to achieve even the minimal degree of reliability required for the protection of any constitutional interest.

DEFICIENCY OF SYSTEM

The first deficiency in Florida's procedure lies in its failure to include the prisoner in the truth-seeking process. Consistent with heightened concern for fairness and accuracy that has characterized our review of the process requisite to the taking of a human life, we believe that any procedure that precludes the prisoner or his counsel from presenting material relevant to his sanity or bars consideration of that material by the fact finder is necessarily inadequate.

A related flaw in the Florida procedure is the denial of any opportunity to challenge or impeach the state-appointed psychiatrists' opinions. Without some questioning of the experts concerning their technical conclusions, a fact finder simply cannot be expected to evaluate the various opinions, particularly when they are themselves inconsistent.

Perhaps the most striking defect in the procedures of Fla Stat § 922.07 (1985 and Supp 1986), as noted earlier, is the State's placement of the decision wholly within the Executive Branch. Under this procedure, the person who appoints the experts and ultimately decides whether the State will be able to carry out the sentence that it has long sought is the Governor, whose subordinates have been responsible for initiating every stage of the prosecution of the condemned from arrest through sentencing. The commander of the State's corps of prosecutors cannot be said to have the neutrality that is necessary for reliability in the fact finding proceeding.

REEXAMINING PROCEDURES

The lodestar of any effort to devise a procedure must be the overriding dual imperative of providing redress for those with substantial claims and of encouraging accuracy in the fact finding determination. The stakes are high, and the "evidence" will always be imprecise. It is all the more important that the adversary presentation of relevant information be as unrestricted as possible. Also essential is that the manner of selecting and using the experts responsible for producing that "evidence" be conducive to the formation of neutral, sound, and professional judgments as to the prisoner's ability to comprehend the nature of the penalty. Fidelity to these principles is the solemn obligation of a civilized society.

Today we have explicitly recognized in our law a principle that has long resided there. It is no less abhorrent today than it has been for centuries to exact in penance the life of one whose mental illness prevents him from comprehending the reasons for the penalty or its implications.

READING

17

EXECUTION OF THE INSANE: THE COUNTERPOINT

Chief Justice William Rehnquist

William H. Rehnquist, Chief Justice of the United States, was born in Milwaukee, Wisconsin, October 1, 1924. He received a B.A., M.A., and L.L.B. from Stanford University and an M.A. from Harvard University. He served as a law clerk for Justice Robert H. Jackson of the Supreme Court of the United States during the 1951 and 1952 Terms, and practiced law in Phoenix, Arizona, from 1953-1969. He served as Assistance Attorney General, Office of Legal Counsel from 1969-1971. President Nixon nominated him to the Supreme Court, and he took his seat as an Associate Justice on January 7, 1972. Nominated as Chief Justice by President Reagan, he assumed that office on September 26, 1986.

■ POINTS TO CONSIDER

1. Why does Justice Rehnquist dissent?

2. How does the majority opinion in Ford v. Wainright undermine rather than uphold our common law heritage according to the Chief Justice?

3. What does Chief Justice Rehnquist say concerning the constitutionality of the death penalty for the insane?

Excerpted from the dissenting opinion of Chief Justice William Rehnquist in the United States Supreme Court decision, **Ford v. Wainright** (1986) 477 US 399, 91 L Ed 2d 335, 106 S Ct 2595.

When the Court creates a constitutional right to a determination of sanity outside of the Executive Branch, it does so not in keeping with but at the expense of "our common law heritage."

The Court today holds that the Eighth Amendment prohibits a state from carrying out a lawfully imposed sentence of death upon a person who is currently insane. This holding is based almost entirely on two unremarkable observations. First, the Court states that it "knows of virtually no authority condoning the execution of the insane in English common law." Second, it notes that "today, no State in the Union permits the execution of the insane." Armed with these facts, and shielded by the claim that it is simply "keeping faith with our common law heritage," the Court proceeds to cast aside settled precedent and to significantly alter both the common law and current practice of not executing the insane. It manages this feat by carefully ignoring the fact that the Florida scheme it finds unconstitutional, in which the Governor is assigned the ultimate responsibility of deciding whether a condemned prisoner is currently insane, is fully consistent with the "common law heritage" and current practice on which the Court purports to rely.

COMMON LAW HERITAGE

The Court places great weight on the "impressive historical credentials" of the common law bar against executing a prisoner who has lost his sanity. What it fails to mention, however, is the equally important and unchallenged fact that under common law it was the executive who passed upon the sanity of the condemned. So when the Court today creates a constitutional right to a determination of sanity outside of the Executive Branch, it does so not in keeping with but at the expense of "our common law heritage."

In Solesbee v. Balkcom (1950), a condemned prisoner claimed that he had a constitutional right to a judicial determination of his sanity. There, as here, the State did not approve the execution of insane persons and vested in the Governor the responsibility for determining, with the aid of experts, the sanity of persons sentenced to death. In rejecting the prisoner's claim, this Court stated:

"Postponement of execution because of insanity bears a close affinity not to trial for a crime but rather to reprieves of sentences in general. The power to reprieve has usually sprung from the same source as the power to pardon. Power of executive clemency in this country undoubtedly derived from the practice as it had existed in England. Such power has traditionally rested in governors or the President, although some of that power is often delegated to agencies such as pardon or parole boards. Seldom, if ever, has this power of executive clemency been subjected to review by the courts."

NO CHANGE CITED

Despite references to "evolving standards of decency," and "the jurisprudence of today," the Court points to no change since Solesbee in the State's approach to determining the sanity of a condemned prisoner. Current statutes quite often provide that initiation of inquiry into and/or final determination of post-sentencing insanity is a matter for the Executive or the prisoner's custodian. The Court's profession of "faith to our common law heritage" and "evolving standards of decency" is thus at best a half-truth. It is Florida's scheme – which combines a prohibition against execution of the insane with Executive Branch procedures for evaluating claims of insanity – that is more faithful to both traditional and modern practice. And no matter how longstanding and universal, laws providing that the State should not execute persons the Executive finds insane are not themselves sufficient to create an Eighth Amendment right that sweeps away as inadequate the procedures for determining sanity crafted by those very laws.

DETERMINING SANITY

The petitioner makes the alternative argument, not reached by the Court, that even if the Eighth Amendment does not prohibit execution of the insane, Florida's decision to bar such executions creates a right in condemned persons to trial-type procedures to determine sanity. Here too, Solesbee is instructive:

"Recently we have pointed out the necessary and inherent differences between trial procedures and post-conviction procedures such as sentencing. Williams v. New York. In that case we emphasized that certain trial procedure safeguards are not applicable to the process of sentencing. This principle applies even more forcefully to an effort to transplant every trial safeguard to a determination of sanity after conviction. As was pointed out in Nobles v. Georgia (1897), to require judicial review every time a

© **Tribune Media Services**, Inc. Reprinted with permission.

convicted defendant suggested insanity would make the possibility of carrying out a sentence depend upon "fecundity in making suggestion after suggestion of insanity." Nobles v. Georgia. To protect itself society must have power to try, convict, and execute sentences. Our legal system demands that this governmental duty be performed with scrupulous fairness to the accused. We cannot say that it offends due process to leave the question of a convicted person's sanity to the solemn responsibility of a state's highest executive with authority to invoke the aid of the most skillful class of experts on the crucial questions involved."

Even the sole dissenter in Solesbee, Justice Frankfurter, agreed that if the Constitution afforded condemned prisoners no substantive right not to be executed when insane, then the State would be free to place on the Governor the responsibility for determining sanity.

The petitioner argues that Solesbee is no longer controlling. But as the petitioner concedes, his due process claim turns on a showing that the Florida statute at issue here created an individual right not to be executed while insane. Even a cursory reading of the statute reveals that the only right it creates in a condemned prisoner is to inform the Governor that the prisoner may be insane. The only legitimate expectation it creates is that "if the Governor decides that the convicted person does not have the mental capacity to understand the nature of the death penalty and why it was imposed on him, he shall have him committed to a Department of Corrections mental health treatment facility." Our recent cases in this area of the law may not be wholly consistent with one another. I do not think this state of the law requires the conclusion that Florida has granted the petitioner the sort of entitlement that gives rise to the procedural protections for which he contends.

EXECUTIVE PROCEDURES SATISFY

In any event, I see no reason to reject the Solesbee Court's conclusion that wholly Executive procedures can satisfy due process in the context of a post-trial, post-appeal, post-collateral-attack challenge to a State's effort to carry out a lawfully imposed sentence. Creating a constitutional right to a judicial determination of sanity before that sentence may be carried out, whether through the Eighth Amendment or the Due Process Clause, needlessly complicates and postpones still further any finality in this area of the law. The defendant has already had a full trial on the issue of penalty; the requirement of still a third adjudication offers an invitation to those who have nothing to lose by accepting it to advance entirely spurious claims of insanity. A claim of insanity may be made at any time before sentence and, once rejected, may be raised again; a prisoner found sane two days before execution might claim to have lost his sanity the next day, thus necessitating another judicial determination of his sanity and presumably another stay of his execution. See Nobles v. Georgia, (1897).

THE REAL BATTLE

Since no state sanctions execution of the insane, the real battle being fought in this case is over what procedures must accompany the inquiry into sanity. The Court reaches the result it does by examining the common law, creating a constitutional right that no state seeks to violate, and then concluding that the common law procedures are inadequate to protect the newly created but common law based right. I find it unnecessary to "constitutionalize" the already uniform view that the insane should not be executed, and inappropriate to "selectively incorporate" the common law practice. I therefore dissent.

READING

18

EXECUTING CHILDREN IS AN UNNECESSARY PRACTICE

Amnesty International, USA

Amnesty International is an independent worldwide organization focused on issues of human rights: the release of prisoners of conscience, fair and prompt trials for political prisoners, and an end to torture and executions.

■ **POINTS TO CONSIDER**

1. Upon what is opposition to the death penalty for minors based?

2. State reasons why adolescence behavior is a poor judge for future behavior, according to this article.

3. Where does U.S. public opinion stand on the issue of executing those who committed crimes as minors?

Excerpted from **United States of America: The Death Penalty and Juvenile Offenders**, Amnesty International, October 1991. Reprinted by permission of Amnesty International, USA 322 Eighth Avenue, New York, NY 10001.

Opposition to the execution of children is based on recognition that minors are not fully mature – hence not fully responsible – and are more likely to be capable of reform, thus rendering the death penalty a particularly inhumane punishment in their cases.

Although the Supreme Court has upheld the death penalty for minors aged 16 and over, a significant body of professional opinion in the USA has rejected the use of capital punishment in such cases.

SCHOLARLY AND LEGAL OPPONENTS

In 1983 the American Bar Association (ABA) House of Delegates adopted a resolution opposing, in principle "...the imposition of capital punishment upon any person for an offense committed while under the age of 18." This was the first time the ABA had taken a formal position on any aspect of capital punishment. Adoption of the resolution followed two years of research by the ABA's Section on Criminal Justice, and their report to the House of Delegates contained a detailed analysis of why the death penalty was inappropriate in such cases. In 1988 the National Council of Juvenile and Family Court Judges also passed a resolution opposing the death penalty for offenders under 18.

As early as 1962, the Model Penal Code drafted by the American Law Institute contained a recommendation that the death penalty not be imposed on persons under 18, a position which was reaffirmed by revisers of the Code in 1980. In 1971 the National Commission on Reform of Federal Criminal Laws also took the position that 18 ought to be the minimum age for the imposition of the death penalty.

A number of other professional and religious organizations have also opposed the imposition of death sentences on minors in *amicus curiae* briefs to the U.S. Supreme Court in juvenile cases. In the Stanford v. Kentucky case (see U.S. Supreme Court rulings above), briefs in support of the petitioners were submitted by numerous organizations, including the ABA; a joint brief by the Child Welfare League of America, National Parents and Teachers Association, National Council on Crime and Delinquency and other bodies; and the American Society for Adolescent Psychiatry and American Orthopsychiatric Association.

Opposition to the execution of children is based on recognition that minors are not fully mature – hence not fully responsible – and are more likely to be capable of reform, thus rendering the death penalty a particularly inhumane punishment in their cases. The reduced culpability of children and adolescents has been generally recognized by criminologists. A Presidential Commission reporting on youth crime in the 1970s observed that "...adolescents, particularly in the early and middle teen years, are more vulnerable, more impulsive, and less self-disciplined than adults. Crimes committed by youths may be just as harmful to victims as those committed by older persons, but they deserve less punishment because adolescents may have less capacity to control their conduct and to think in long-range terms than adults..."

RETRIBUTION AND DETERRENCE

It has also been argued that the goals of retribution or deterrence – arguments commonly used to support the death penalty – are especially inapplicable in the case of young people, who are more likely to act on impulse, or under the domination or influence of others, with little thought for the long-term consequences of their actions.

Citing the findings of the report by its Section on Criminal Justice in its brief in Stanford v. Kentucky, the ABA said "...in light of the characteristics associated with childhood – impulsiveness, lack of self control, poor judgment, feelings of invincibility – the deterrent value of the juvenile death penalty is likely of little consequence...in any event, it would be difficult to support a claim that the death penalty as a deterrent for juvenile crime, as opposed to life imprisonment, "is an indispensable part of the State's criminal justice system."

Criminologists and others who have studied the application of the death penalty in juvenile cases have also noted that many juveniles convicted of terrible crimes themselves come from brutalizing and deprived backgrounds. This was borne out in a recent study by psychiatrists of juveniles under sentence of death in four U.S. states in the 1980s. It has been argued that to execute such offenders, whether as retribution or as an intended deterrent, is not only inhumane but denies the special responsibility which society has toward children.

138

NOT IN GOOD COMPANY

The USA carries out more executions of juvenile offenders (people sentenced to death for a crime they committed when they were under the age of 18) than almost any other country in the world.

"United States of America: Developments in the Death Penalty during 1993." **Amnesty International, USA,** New York: March 1994.

Appeals against the execution of juvenile offenders have also pointed out that a child's capacity for development continues throughout adolescence, making it impossible to make firm predictions about his or her future behavior. A petition to the U.S. Supreme Court in the case of 15-year-old offender William Wayne Thompson quoted from the American Psychiatric Association's diagnostic guide to mental disorders, which states: "...Since the typical childhood signs of antisocial personality disorder may terminate spontaneously..., a diagnosis of antisocial personality disorder should not be made in children; it is reserved for adults (18 or over), who have had time to show the full longitudinal pattern."

MISLEADING DIAGNOSIS

Despite this, however, death sentences have been imposed on juvenile offenders on the basis of such a diagnosis, together with a finding that they are likely to be dangerous in the future. This applies particularly to cases in Texas, whose capital punishment statute requires juries to impose a death sentence on the finding (with two other circumstances) that there is a probability of the defendant committing "criminal acts of violence that would constitute a continuing threat to society."

Cases submitted to the U.S. Supreme Court have also argued that U.S. law in many other areas recognizes that children under 18 are inherently less responsible than adults. In all U.S. states and the District of Columbia, 18 is the minimum age, for example, at which a person may vote or sit on a jury. In 49 states the age of majority is 18 years or older. Most states place numerous other restriction on persons under 18 (regarding, for example, the right to purchase alcohol, to gamble, to marry, drive a car or join the armed forces without parental consent). It has been argued that this general recognition of the lesser responsibility of minors should be reflected in the criminal law – at least to the extent that the ultimate penalty of death should not be applied in such cases.

It has also been pointed out that, far from being more responsible than the average teenager, juvenile offenders are typically below their chronological age in terms of intelligence and emotional maturity, a factor confirmed in the cases reviewed by Amnesty International. Justice Brennan, writing for the dissent in Stanford v. Kentucky commented that "...insofar as age 18 is a necessarily arbitrary social choice as a point at which to acknowledge a person's maturity and responsibility, given the different developmental rates of individuals, it is in fact a conservative estimate of the dividing line between adolescence and adulthood. Many of the psychological and emotional changes that an adolescent experiences in maturing do not actually occur until the early 20s." Brief for the American Society for Adolescent Psychiatry and American Orthopsychiatric Association as Amici Curiae 4 (citing social studies).

U.S. PUBLIC OPINION

Public opinion in the USA may be said generally to favor retention of the death penalty. However, in an opinion poll conducted in Tennessee and Georgia in December, 1985, more than two to one of those polled opposed the execution of juveniles aged under 18 at the time of the crime. (The poll was conducted by the University of Georgia; 400 registered voters were polled in each of the towns of Macon (Georgia) and Nashville (Tennessee), areas where support for the death penalty in general is reported to be high.) A telephone survey of 509 respondents in Connecticut carried out in May, 1986 showed that, while 68% favored the death penalty in general, only 31% supported it for crimes committed by offenders under 18.

140

READING

19

EXECUTING CHILDREN: LET THE STATES DECIDE WHAT IS CRUEL AND UNUSUAL

James J. Kilpatrick

James J. Kilpatrick is a nationally syndicated columnist and regular observer of courts and the judicial process.

■ POINTS TO CONSIDER

1. What was the question left open to the Supreme Court in the summer of 1989?

2. Discuss the opinion in the Stanford case that the majority of the court held.

3. Why does this demonstrate jurisprudence at its best for Kilpatrick?

4. Contrast Justices Scalia and Frankfurter with Justices Brennan and Warren in deciding what dictates standards of decency.

The significance of the Supreme Court's opinion lies not so much in the bright line that it draws at age 16. The states have it within their power to draw the line on capital punishment at 17 or 18 if they wish.

Kevin Stanford was 17 years and four months of age when he murdered a woman in Kentucky. Heath Wilkins was 16 years and six months of age when he murdered a woman in Missouri. Both were tried as adults, convicted and sentenced to death. On June 26, 1989, the Supreme Court voted 5-4 to let the executions proceed.

In both cases the constitutional question was the same: is it cruel and unusual punishment, in violation of the Eighth Amendment, to impose a death sentence upon persons who were under the age of 18 when their crimes were committed? A majority of the court said no, it is not. At least it was not unconstitutional in the summer of 1989.

BRUTAL CRIMES

These were brutal crimes. Stanford and an accomplice found their victim at a gas station where she worked. The two of them repeatedly raped and sodomized her. "They then drove her to a secluded area near the station, where Stanford shot her point-blank in the face and then in the back of her head." A corrections officer testified that Stanford said he had to shoot her because she lived next door and would recognize him. After he described the crime, "he started laughing."

For his part, young Wilkins and an accomplice targeted 26-year-old Nancy Allen, mother of two infant children, as she worked behind the counter of a convenience store in Avondale, MO. Wilkins intended murder from the beginning. He stabbed her repeatedly while his accomplice raided the cash register. "When Allen began to beg for her life, Wilkins stabbed her four more times in the neck, opening her carotid artery."

JUDICIAL RESTRAINT

So much for the facts. The significance of the Supreme Court's opinion lies not so much in the bright line that it draws at age 16. The states have it within their power to draw the line on capital punishment at 17 or 18 if they wish. The important thing about

NOTHING NEW

Legally sanctioned juvenile executions came to this country via English law. Through its long, turbulent history, and until 1908 (the United Kingdom abolished capital punishment in 1969) England legally sanctioned execution of teens and pre-teens for such crimes as picking pockets, theft, rape, murder. However, actually executing juveniles in England was a rare occurrence. "Research at Old Bailey revealed that although more than one hundred youths had been sentenced to death from 1801 to 1836, none had been executed. While some cases do exist, it appears settled that execution of youths was never at any time common in England." (Streib, 1995)

Executing children in the United States has been similarly rare. Although many have been sentenced to death by juries, the commutation rate has been very high. From the 1890s through the 1920s, the number of juvenile offenders executed ranged from 20 to 27 per decade – 1.6 to 2.3 percent of all executions. In the 1930s executions hit an all-time high, 1,670 for the decade. During this same decade, juvenile offender executions also rose to 41; still that was only 2.5 percent.

While review of historical data reveals that executing a juvenile offender has never been a popular practice, killing kids in this country is not new. The first documented juvenile execution occurred in Roxbury, Massachusetts, in 1642. Sixteen-year-old Thomas Graunger was hanged for the crime of bestiality. The youth, who sodomized a horse and cow, was convicted by a jury of adult males and sentenced under the Old Testament law described in Leviticus 20:15.

Nelson, Lane. "Killing Kids." **The Angolite.** Nov./Dec. 1995.

this case is the example it provides of judicial restraint. This was jurisprudence at its best.

Justice Antonin Scalia, speaking for the majority, began by examining the doctrine of "original intent." Manifestly the execution of 16- or 17-year-olds was not unconstitutional when the

Eighth Amendment was adopted in 1791. "At that time, the common law theoretically permitted capital punishment to be imposed on anyone over the age of seven."

Just as obviously, interpretation of "cruel and unusual" has changed over the years. Thirty-four years ago the court laid down some guidelines. The case involved a wartime deserter, Albert Trop, who had been convicted by court-martial and stripped of his nationality and his citizenship. Was this punishment a violation of the Eighth Amendment? Speaking through Chief Justice Earl Warren, five justices agreed that it was.

"The words of the amendment are not precise," said Warren, "and their scope is not static. The amendment must draw its meaning from the evolving standards of decency that mark the progress of a maturity society."

Very well. But how is a court to determine what standards of decency have evolved at any given time? The temptation is for justices simply to apply their own standards of decency. This Scalia refused to do. "Judgment should be informed by objective factors to the maximum possible extent." Therefore he looked to the people through their state legislatures.

Of the 37 states that authorize capital punishment, 15 decline to impose it upon 16-year-olds and another three decline to impose it on 17-year-olds. The other 19 states authorize executions for crimes committed at age 16 or above. In those legislative acts lies the best evidence of "evolving standards of decency."

PHILOSOPHER-KINGS

The four dissenters, led by Justice William Brennan, brushed aside this line of reasoning. In their view, members of the Supreme Court should apply their own notion of what punishment is decent or "proportionate." Justices should decide for themselves if a death sentence contributes measurably to "acceptable goals of punishment."

Scalia had the last word. To adopt the Brennan view of the power of judges, he said, "is to replace judges of the law with a committee of philosopher-kings."

Remarkably, Justice Felix Frankfurter said about the same thing in the Trop case involving the wartime deserter. Justices must not give effect "to their own notions of what is wise and politic."

Such policy decisions should not be left to five unelected and life-tenured judges. They ought to be left to the states respectively, or to the people.

READING

20

THE GENDER GAP ON DEATH ROW

Victor L. Streib

Victor L. Streib is a professor of Law at Pettit College of Law at Ohio Northern University. The author began compiling reports monitoring the death penalty and female offenders in 1988. He was formerly Professor of Law at Cleveland-Marshall College of Law at Cleveland State University.

■ POINTS TO CONSIDER

1. How prevalent have executions of women been throughout American history?

2. In the modern era of capital sentencing (1973-present) how likely is it for a woman to be executed? What is the reversal rate for females sentenced to death?

3. According to the author, what is the most common offense for women sentenced to death?

4. Despite high reversal rates, does the author believe that an execution of a female will occur in the future? Why or why not?

In general, both the female death sentencing rate and the female death row population remain very small in comparison to that for males. Actual execution of female offenders is quite rare.

This report documents twenty-three and one-half years of the death sentencing of females offenders under modern death penalty statutes in the United States. In 1988 I began to generate these reports in order to monitor this phenomenon...

As of this writing, the death penalty for women is back in the headlines. The state of South Carolina unsuccessfully sought the death penalty for Susan Smith, convicted of having drowned her young children last year. This was an unusual case, in that the death penalty for a mother who murders her own children is quite rare. Only eleven (10%) of the 113 death sentences imposed upon female offenders since 1973 have been for the murder of their own children, and only six (13%) of the forty-six women offenders now under death sentences have been sentenced to death for such crimes.

Attention was also drawn to the case of Pamela Perillo in Texas, who had been scheduled for execution in September, 1995, and again early in 1996. This scheduled execution was delayed when an appellate court granted another hearing in Perillo's case. Another prominent case in the news was that of Guinevere Garcia in Illinois, scheduled originally to be executed on January 17, 1996. Garcia had been under a death sentence for only just over three years, making her one of the more recent additions to the death row for women. Garcia steadfastly refused to fight her death sentence and repeatedly asked to be executed as soon as possible. However, only a few hours before her scheduled execution, the Governor of Illinois commuted her sentence to life imprisonment. Neither Perillo nor Garcia was executed, but the actual execution of another woman in the United States seems likely to occur in the next year or two.

ACTUAL EXECUTION OF WOMEN

In general, both the female death sentencing rate and the female death row population remain very small in comparison to that for males. Actual execution of female offenders is quite rare, with only 514 documented instances beginning with the first in 1632. These 514 female executions constitute less than 3% of the total of 18,922 confirmed executions in the United States since 1608. The last female offender executed was Velma Barfield in North Carolina on November 2, 1984, the only female among about 330 offenders executed in the post-Furman era (1973 - present). Prior to this current era, the last female offender executed was Elizabeth Ann Duncan, executed by California on August 8, 1962. The annual rate of death sentences for female offenders has remained around five or six (2% of the annual total) for many years.

Death sentences and actual executions for female offenders are also rare in comparison to such events for male offenders. In fact, women are more likely to be dropped out of the system the further the capital punishment system progresses. Following in summary outline form are the data indicating this screening out effect:

• Women account for about one in eight (13%) murder arrests;

• Women account for only one in fifty (2%) death sentences imposed at the trial level;

• Women account for only one in seventy (1.5%) persons presently on death row; and

• Women account for only one in 330 (0.3%) persons actually executed in this modern era.

In sum, women are unlikely to be arrested for murder, extremely unlikely to be sentenced to death, and almost never executed.

CURRENT ERA

The current American death penalty era began when new death penalty statutes were passed following the Supreme Court's decision in Furman in 1972, which in effect struck down all then-existing death penalty statutes. Sentencing began under the new statutes in 1973 and continues through today. Although the constitutionality of these current era statutes was not recognized formally by the United States Supreme Court until 1976 in Gregg and actual executions did not begin until 1977, the current era of sentencing began in 1973.

Table 1 lists the sentences imposed each year according to the Bureau of Justice Statistics and to my research. A total of 113 female death sentences have been imposed, about 2% of the total of estimated 5,730 death sentences for all offenders. Despite

Table 1
Death Sentences Imposed Upon Female Offenders,
January 1, 1973, to June 30, 1996

Year	Total Death Sentences*	Female Death Sentences	Portion of Total
1973	42	1	2.4%
1974	149	1	0.7%
1975	298	7	2.3%
1976	234	3	1.3%
1977	138	1	0.7%
1978	187	4	2.1%
1979	156	4	2.6%
1980	182	2	1.1%
1981	233	3	1.3%
1982	272	5	1.8%
1983	253	4	1.6%
1984	287	8	2.8%
1985	277	5	1.8%
1986	306	3	1.0%
1987	290	5	1.7%
1988	295	5	1.7%
1989	264	11	4.2%
1990	256	7	2.7%
1991	277	6	2.2%
1992	285	10	3.5%
1993	295	6	2.0%
1994	304	5	1.6%
1995	300**	7	2.3%
1996***	150**	0	0.0%
Totals:	**5,730****	**113**	**2.0%**

* Source of data: U.S. Dept. of Justice, Capital Punishment 1994 at 12, appendix table 1 (1996).

** Estimates

*** As of June 30

IF IT'S OK TO EXECUTE 21·YEAR·OLDS, THEN WHY NOT 18·YEAR·OLDS? IF IT'S OK TO EXECUTE 18·YEAR·OLDS, THEN WHY NOT 16·YEAR·OLDS? IF IT'S OK TO EXECUTE 16·YEAR·OLDS, THEN.......

Reprinted with permission from the **Star Tribune**, Minneapolis.

some fluctuations particularly in the early years of this period, the death sentencing rate for female offenders was typically about five per year beginning in the 1980s. In 1989 this annual death sentencing rate doubled for reasons unknown. In 1990 and 1991, the sentencing rate seemed to have returned to just above the pre-1989 levels. Then the rate surged to ten in 1992, portending an annual rate again nearly double that of the 1980s. This is nearly 4% of the death sentences imposed in 1992, suggesting a significant increase in the rate of the death sentencing of female offenders. However, four of these ten female death sentences in 1992 were imposed on the same person (Aileen Wuornos in Florida), leaving only six other female death sentences during 1992. Total female death sentences then returned to the normal level – six in 1993, five in 1994, and seven in 1995. In any event, the number of female offenders sentenced to prison death rows each year remains under 0.2% of the approximately 3,700 women sentenced to prison each year.

Of these 113 death sentences for female offenders, only forty-six sentences remain currently in effect (see Table 3). One such sentence resulted in an execution (Velma Barfield) and another sixty-six death sentences were reversed or commuted to life imprisonment. Thus, for the sixty-seven death sentences finally resolved

GENDER BIAS

Another surprising discovery about the executions of female offenders is the remarkable decline in this practice during this century...only thirty-nine females have been executed in this century, less than in any century in our past...

Actual execution of female offenders continues to be a very rare phenomenon. The last female offender executed was Velma Barfield in North Carolina on November 2, 1984, the only female among 174 offenders executed thus far in the current era...

The death penalty for female offenders continues to be a very rare threat through the current American practice of imposing the death penalty for murder. It always has been so. While reluctant to be cast in the role of urging states to terminate the lives of several more wretched sisters in order to achieve gender parity, one must be suspicious of the extraordinarily low rate of death sentences and executions for female offenders. More would have been expected, absent some inherent gender bias in the capital punishment system.

Victor L. Streib, "Death Penalty for Battered Women," **Florida State University Law Review**, Summer, 1992.

(excluding the forty-six still in effect and still being litigated), the reversal rate for female death sentences in the current era is 99% (66/67).

These 113 death sentences for female offenders have been imposed in twenty-three individual states, comprising well over half of the death penalty jurisdictions during this time period. Table 2 lists all death penalty jurisdictions which have imposed death sentences on female offenders since 1973.

As Table 2 indicates, two states (Florida and North Carolina) account for nearly one-quarter of all such sentences. The first ten states have imposed three-quarters of female death sentences. These dominant sentencing states range from North Carolina to California and from Texas and Florida to Ohio...

151

Table 2

State-By-State Breakdown of Death Sentences for Females,
January 1, 1973 to June 30, 1996

| Rank | Sentencing State | Race of Offender | | | | Total Female Sentences |
		White	Black	Latino	American Indian	
1	Florida	11	3	1	0	15
2	North Carolina	8	3	0	1	12
3	California	4	3	2	0	9
	Ohio	3	6	0	0	9
	Texas	7	2	0	0	9
6	Alabama	5	2	0	0	7
	Oklahoma	6	1	0	0	7
8	Mississippi	4	2	0	0	6
9	Georgia	4	1	0	0	5
	Illinois	1	3	1	0	5
	Missouri	4	0	1	0	5
12	Indiana	2	2	0	0	4
	Pennsylvania	1	3	0	0	4
14	Maryland	1	0	0	2	3
15	Idaho	2	0	0	0	2
	Kentucky	2	0	0	0	2
	Louisiana	1	1	0	0	2
	Nevada	1	1	0	0	2
19	Arizona	1	0	0	0	1
	New Jersey	1	0	0	0	1
	South Carolina	1	0	0	0	1
	Tennessee	1	0	0	0	1
	Totals	**72**	**33**	**5**	**3**	**113**

CURRENT FEMALE DEATH ROW INMATES

Of the 113 death sentences imposed since 1973, only forty-six
females remain on the death rows of fifteen states (see Table 3).
These forty-six female offenders on death row constitute only
1.5% of the total death row population of about 3,070 persons
and less than 0.1% of the approximately 50,000 women in prison
in the United States.

Table 3
Characteristics of Offenders and Victims in Female Death Penalty
Cases Currently in Force, June 30, 1996

Offenders

Age at Crime				Race			
Under 21	=	5	(11%)	B	=	16	(35%)
21-30	=	17	(37%)	L	=	3	(7%)
31-40	=	12	(26%)	W	=	27	(59%)
41-50	=	7	(15%)			46	(100%)
51-60	=	4	(9%)				
61-70	=	1	(1%)				
		46	(100%)				

Victims

Age			Race				Sex			
Under 18 =	14	(24%)	A	=	3	(5%)	M	=	43	(66%)
18 & over =	45	(76%)	B	=	12	(19%)	F	=	22	(34%)
	59	(100%)	L	=	7	(11%)			65	(100%)
Unknown =	9		W	=	41	(65%)	Unknown	=	3	
	68				63	(100%)			68	
			Unknown	=	5					
					68					

Well over one-half of the women on death row are white. One fourth were in their forties or older at the time of their crimes, with the total age range remarkably from eighteen to sixty-seven. Two-thirds of their victims were white, and two-thirds were adult males (where these data are known). The most typical crimes of these women involved the murder of the offender's husband or lover. Several of these female offenders were battered women who killed their batterers or victims chosen by their batterers.

The present ages of these forty-six female death row inmates range from twenty-two to seventy-seven years old. They have been on death row from one to fourteen years. Despite the statistically high probability (99%) that death-sentenced female offenders will never be executed, some of these women have nearly exhausted appeals. Another execution of a female offender seems likely within the next few years.

READING

21

NO GENDER GAP ON DEATH ROW

Elizabeth Rapaport

Elizabeth Rapaport is known for her writings on gender bias and the death penalty. The following article was excerpted from the Law and Society Review *at the University of Massachusetts.*

■ POINTS TO CONSIDER

1. Summarize the two hypotheses Rapaport states for explaining the underrepresentation of women on death row.

2. Discuss the types of crimes women commit. How does this compare to the crimes committed by men?

3. What kind of crimes are most frequently subject to capital sentencing? The majority of those crimes are committed by whom?

4. According to the author, how is the peace of the domestic sphere (family relations) devalued by our current capital sentencing scheme? How is this "patriarchal?"

Excerpted from Elizabeth Rapaport. "The Death Penalty and Gender Discrimination," **Law and Society Review**. vol. 25, no. 2 1991: 367-83. Reprinted by permission of the Law and Society Association.

There is, from a feminist point of view, an invidious subordination of the interests of women involved in the failure of the statutes to attach our society's most profound condemnation to crimes that destroy the domestic peace.

It would seem, superficially at least, that if there is gender discrimination in the U.S. capital punishment regime, it favors female offenders. At most, two percent of those executed from colonial times to the present have been female (Bedau 1982:3). In the modern death penalty era, which begins with the Supreme Court's constitutional invalidation of then existing capital statutory schemes in 1972 and the imposition of novel constitutional requirements on the fashioning of such statutes in 1976, approximately two percent of those condemned have been female. Only one woman has been among the 143 persons executed since executions resumed in 1977, after a decade-long moratorium during which the future of capital punishment in the United States had been in doubt (NAACP Legal Defense and Educational Fund 1991:1). A gross comparison of the death-sentencing rates for men and women suggests that women convicted of murder are underrepresented on death row. Two percent of men but only one tenth of one percent of women convicted of murder are condemned to die.

For a feminist to raise the issue of gender discrimination and capital punishment is not an altogether comfortable undertaking. At worst, it suggests a campaign to exterminate a few more wretched sisters. In my view, however, the issue is worth confronting. The reputed leniency that women receive with respect to death sentencing supports the view widely held in our society that women are incapable of achieving, nor are they in fact held to, the same standards of personal responsibility as are men...

There has been very little research on the death penalty and gender discrimination, either before or after the Supreme Court mandated a new constitutional regime for the administration of capital punishment in 1976; yet the charge that women receive favorable treatment has been aired, notably by Justice Marshall in his concurring opinion in Furman v. Georgia (1972), in which he asks, rhetorically, how the disparity between the number of murders women commit and the number of women executed can be explained other than by discrimination in favor of women.

TWO HYPOTHESES

Does the sparseness of women on death row result from a chivalrous disinclination to mete out death to women under circumstances in which men would be consigned to this fate? Or does the apparent underrepresentation of women have an explanation other than gender discrimination in our favor? Two hypotheses, singly or in combination, would account for the gender profile of America's death rows: (1) women offenders are benefiting from gender discrimination in their favor; (2) women are represented on death row in numbers commensurate with the infrequency of female commission of those crimes our society labels sufficiently reprehensible to merit capital punishment.

In the first part of this article I explore what currently available information can tell us about the extent of gender discrimination in selection for death. I then offer a profile of condemned men and women in order to compare the crimes and the characteristics of male and female capital offenders. The question explored there is whether men and women are selected for the most severe sanction our society can impose for the same or different sorts of reasons. In the final part I discuss a form of gender discrimination built into U.S. death penalty law that expresses and reinforces the subordination of women: under modern era law, the death penalty is a possible punishment only for crimes and criminals that evoke our society's most extreme condemnation. The crimes whose prohibition we solemnize by treating as death-eligible are those which, overwhelmingly, are predatory crimes committed by men against other men or against women and children not their own. The death penalty, therefore, is a dramatic symbol of the lesser dignity attached to the security and peace of the domestic sphere as compared with the realms of commerce and intercourse among non-intimates.

According to FBI Supplementary Homicide Reports (SHR) data, in the twelve years 1976-87, women made up 14.3 percent of murder and non-negligent manslaughter suspects known to the police. If women commit 14 percent of all such killings, they commit substantially fewer of those murders that are subjected to capital adjudication. The great majority of capital sentences are meted out to those who have committed felony murder, murder committed during the course of another serious felony, and other predatory murders. More than 80 percent of the death sentences in some jurisdictions that have been studied are pronounced on

156

"The world's first solar-powered electric chair. Now THAT should satisfy the liberals."

Cartoon by Carol ★ Simpson. Reprinted with permission.

felony murderers; nationally the percentage exceeds 75 percent. Women seldom commit felony murders. Of 20,905 persons suspected by the police of committing felony murders of rape, burglary, robbery, auto theft, arson, and the catch-all category of other felony for 1976-87, only 6.2 percent were women.

Most murders, whether committed by men or women, are not sufficiently aggravated to tempt prosecutors to pursue a death penalty. An important reason why so few women are eligible for capital sentences is that women who kill are more likely than men to kill family and other intimates in anger rather than to kill for a predatory purpose. Predatory murder is committed to gain some material or other advantage, in contrast with killing that appears to be stimulated by powerful emotion. Felony and other predatory murders are most often committed against strangers and least often committed against family and other intimates. The victims of women killers are substantially more likely than those of men to be family members and less likely to be strangers...

SELECTION FOR DEATH

Three factors that legitimately influence selection for death, then, are prior criminal record, offense seriousness, and degree of culpability. There are indications that at least two of these factors, prior record and offense seriousness, legitimately expose more male than female murderers to capital sentencing.

A majority of death penalty states treat prior history of violence as a factor in aggravation of murder which, if not outweighed by mitigating factors, permits a jury to impose the death penalty. Such factors as prior felony conviction, prior history of violence, and prior conviction for murder express the condemnation of a history of violence common in the capital statutes. Male murderers with prior convictions for a violent felony are substantially more likely to face trial than are female murderers with a comparable record. Twenty percent of male murderers but only five percent of female murderers convicted in state courts in 1986 had a prior conviction for a violent felony. Thus male murderers were four times more likely to possess a disadvantageous prior history that would induce a prosecutor to seek a capital trial and a jury to impose a death sentence.

An important measure of offense seriousness as interpreted by modern death penalty statutes is the amount of violence or brutality employed by the offender. The statutes stigmatize excessive violence and attempt to measure it by asking juries to consider such factors as whether the murder was brutal, whether torture was employed, whether persons other than the victims were placed at grave risk, and whether more than one victim perished. Men are demonstrably more prone than women to commit violent crime.

Although multiple homicides are quite rare, they are substantially more likely to lead to death sentences than are single victim killings. In the twelve-year period 1976-87, only 7.2 percent of multiple murder suspects were female, again suggesting that one should not expect female death sentences to approach the 14 percent mark reflecting female involvement in murder of every category.

Finally, there is the question of the relative culpability of male and female murderers. If female perpetrators of felony murders and other predatory murders are legitimately perceived as being less culpable than similar males, women should legitimately receive fewer death sentences than male murderers. For example, if women who figure in multiple perpetrator felony murders (most robbery murders are multiple perpetrator crimes; see Block 1985: 18) are commonly mere accomplices of men, one would expect a lower rate of death sentences for female robbery murderers. Relative culpability is much in need of further study, since it is an area in which at present we have little to guide us except unexamined stereotypical thinking. Common sense would incline many observers to suppose that women are often both perceived by prosecutors and juries to be, and objectively are, mere accomplices of dominant males...

CHIVALRY IS DEAD

The explanation for much, if not all, of the apparent disparity between the proportion of murderers who are women and the proportion of women on death row is not chivalrous regard for the female sex. It is to be found in the differences between the kinds of murders men and women commit and the kinds of personal history they present to prosecutors and sentencers: female murderers are dramatically less likely than male murderers to have committed predatory murder and to appear in the dock as habitual and exceptionally violent felons. The sparseness of women on death row more reflects our society's judgments about the nature of the most reprehensible and hence most severely sanctioned crimes than our protectiveness of women...

Analysis reveals that three broad categories of murders are stigmatized as death-eligible in the death penalty statutes of this type: (1) predatory murder, (2) murder that hinders or threatens the enforcement of law or other governmental functions, and (3) murder that evinces excessive violence or brutality...

159

The worst cases of domestic violence, unlike the worst cases of robbery violence, are not, as such, eligible for capital adjudication. Domestic crimes may nonetheless become capital cases if they are regarded as especially brutal crimes or if they are also pecuniary crimes. But the paradigmatic domestic killing, arising out of hot anger at someone who is capable, as it were by definition, of calling out painful and sudden emotion in his or her killer, is virtually the antithesis of a capital murder. Yet there are features of domestic homicides that could plausibly be regarded as among the most reprehensible crimes: they involve the betrayal of familial trust and responsibility on which not only domestic peace but presumably our civilization depends, as much it depends on honoring the law of mine and thine and respecting the authority of the state. They also have characteristics that could be read as inherent extreme brutality. The victims of family murders are typically especially vulnerable to their killers because of physical weakness and psychological dependency. Often the victims have been the objects of prior and habitual violence by their killers.

Whether or not one endorses or opposes capital punishment on moral or other grounds, and whether or not one would wish to see its domain enlarged for any purpose, there is, from a feminist point of view, an invidious subordination of the interests of women involved in the failure of the statutes to attach our society's most profound condemnation to crimes that destroy the domestic peace. These murders are also far more likely to have women and children as victims than are economic crimes. Our law reveals a disposition to regard killing a stranger for gain as more heinous than killing a spouse or child in anger. This both privileges the interests of men over those of women and children and supports patriarchal values...

CONCLUSION

It may well be that the underevaluation of the heinousness of domestic murder is the most serious form of gender discrimination to be discovered in our capital punishment system. In the present state of our knowledge, I have tried to show, we have no credible evidence that women are spared the death penalty in circumstances where it would be pronounced on men. The gender composition of death row rather appears to reflect differences between the kinds of homicides men and women commit. Additionally, there is some evidence that the admissions standards for death

160

row may be somewhat different for the two sexes. Although women are indeed sent to death row for crimes that lead men to the same fate, a strikingly high percentage of the women on death row, unlike the men, killed family or intimates. The question of the death penalty and gender discrimination, then, appears to be fundamentally a question of social ideology. Women are doubly disserved by the current climate of belief and policy. First, women are disserved by the misleading or false belief that we are spared the most extreme criminal sanction because of our sex. Second, the criminal law is not being mobilized to sufficiently discredit, discourage, and sanction crimes of domestic oppression from which women and children suffer disproportionately.

HABEAS CORPUS & THE ANTI-TERRORISM AND EFFECTIVE DEATH PENALTY ACT OF 1996: AN OVERVIEW[1]

Passage of the Anti-terrorism and Effective Death Penalty Act of 1996, Pub. L.No. 104-132, 110 Stat. 1214 (April 24, 1996) marks the end of the most recent round of debate over federal *habeas corpus.* Federal *habeas corpus* is the statutory procedure, 28 U.S.C. 2241 et seq., under which state and federal prisoners may petition the federal courts to review their convictions and sentences to determine whether they are contrary to the laws or Constitution of the United States.

Federal *habeas* has been characterized as an important safeguard against constitutional violations in the area of criminal procedure and, alternatively, as a waste of time, a threat to federalism, and harmful to our system of criminal justice.

At common law, the writ we know as *habeas corpus* was a judicial procedure whereby prisoners, held without trial, without being admitted to bail, or confined by order of court without subject matter jurisdiction, might secure their release. The writ was not available to those convicted by courts with jurisdiction.

Federal *habeas* underwent considerable statutory and judicial expansion until the late 1960s when concerns of federalism and finality led the Supreme Court to restrict state prisoner access to the writ. The procedure, nevertheless, was still blamed for delays in state capital punishment cases. A committee, chaired by retired Justice Powell, recommended changes to deal with the delays. Some critics of that approach urged a return to the direction of the law in the late 60s; others contended the Powell

[1]Excerpted from Charles Doyle, Congressional Reference Report for Congress, May 14, 1996.

Committee recommendations should be carried further. Congress had studied variations of proposed *habeas* revision for at least fifteen years.

SUMMARY

The Anti-terrorism and Effective Death Penalty Act of 1996, Pub.L.No. 104-132, 110 Stat. 1214 (April 24, 1996) substantially revises federal *habeas corpus*.

In the case of both death row inmates and other prisoners, the Act:

- establishes a one-year deadline within which state prisoners must file their federal *habeas* petitions

- narrows the circumstances under which a federal or state prisoner may appeal a federal district court's denial of his or her petition for *habeas* relief

- bars federal *habeas* relief to state prisoners whose claims have been decided by the state courts unless the result was contrary to U.S. Supreme Court precedent or was based upon an unreasonable finding of fact

- amends *habeas* procedure for federal prisoners to include the one-year statute of limitations, attorneys' fees, and limitations on successive petitions which the Act makes applicable to the *habeas* procedure for state prisoners

- bars repetitious *habeas* petitions by state and federal prisoners.

In the case of state death row inmates, the Act streamlines federal *habeas* procedures in states that have a system for the appointment and compensation of attorneys who represent indigent state prisoners in state collateral review or unitary review proceedings. Streamlining for the states that opt in, include:

- a one-time automatic stay of execution and a 180-day statute of limitations

- a limit on *habeas* review to issues raised and decided on the merits in state court

- a right to a determination by the district court within 120 days and by the federal court of appeals within 120 days.

The statute also eliminates the automatic *ex parte* nature of the request and approval of investigative, expert and other services available to indigent death row inmates in connection with the presentation of their federal *habeas corpus* petitions.

INDEX

BIBLIOGRAPHY

Magazine References

Anderson, Charles Edward. "Low IQ Murderers: States Seek Executions of Mentally Retarded Convicts." **American Bar Association Journal**, Oct. 1989.

Anderson, George M. "Capital Punishment in Perspective: An Interview with Kevin Doyle, Manager of the New York State Capital Defender Office." **America**, April 20, 1996: 16.

Anderson, George M. "Jail and Prison Ministry." **America**, Aug. 17, 1996: 6.

"At Death Row's Door." **The Lawyer**, July 23, 1996: 17.

Barnes, Patricia G. "States Allow Victims' Families to Watch Executions." **American Bar Association Journal**, March 1996.

Bonnie, Richard J. "The Death Penalty: When Doctors Must Say No." **British Medical Journal**, Aug. 15, 1992: 381.

Butler, Paul. "Racially Based Jury Nullification: Black Power in the Criminal Justice System." **Yale Law Journal**, Dec. 1995: 677-725.

Carbonara, Peter. "Drawing the Line on Death Row Appeals." **The American Lawyer**, Nov. 1992: 106.

Carro, Jorge L. "Capital Punishment from a Global Perspective." **Vital Speeches**, Aug. 1, 1996: 629.

Cole, David. "Courting Capital Punishment: With Little Public Opposition, the Machinery of Death Is Shifting into Overdrive." **The Nation**, Feb. 26, 1996: 20.

Collins, Chris. "First to Propose Death for Drug Dealers." **The Montgomery Advertiser**, Feb. 11, 1996.

"Death Penalty Debate." **The American Lawyer**, May 1994: 10.

Devito, Paul L. & Ralph Hyatt. "What Constitutes 'Appropriate Punishment'?" **USA Today**, March 1995: 89.

Dispoldo, Nick. "Capital Punishment and the Poor." **America**, Feb. 11, 1995: 18.

Ellis, David. "Tommy Pope Wants to Send Child Killer Susan Smith to the Electric Chair." **People**, Jan. 30, 1995: 76.

Evans, Kathy. Beheaded for brewing beer; Saudi Arabia had an increase in beheading sentences during the last five years including 90 people killed in the first quarter of 1995, mainly foreign workers. **World Press Review**, July 1995: 38.

Frame, Randy. "A Matter of Life and Death: As the Number of Executions Surges." **Christianity Today**, Aug. 14, 1995: 50.

Gest, Ted. "Crime's Bias Problem." **U.S. News & World Report**, July 25, 1994: 31.

Gleick, Elizabeth. "Rich Justice, Poor Justice; Did We Need O.J. to Remind Us That Money Makes All the Difference – in the Trial?" **Time**, June 19, 1995: 40.

Grant, Meg. "Bryan Stevenson; A Stubborn Alabama Lawyer Stands Alone Between Death and His Clients." **People**, Nov. 27, 1995: 71.

Hansen, Mark. "Commuted Death Sentence Raises Question Whether Females Are Treated More Leniently." **American Bar Association Journal**, April 1996.

Haywood, Richette L. "Is the Death Penalty Fair to Blacks?" **Jet**, March 13, 1995: 12.

"Innocent on Death Row." **America**, Jan. 13, 1996: 3.

Jerome, Richard. "No Reprieve; Seventeen Years After Intruders Murdered Their Parents." **People**, Aug. 26, 1996: 42.

Keeva, Steven. "Justice on Death Row." **American Bar Association Journal**, April 1996.

Klein, Marty. "Sex, Crime & Punishment: Are We Willing to Rehabilitate Sexually Dangerous People?" **Playboy**, May 1995: 44.

Lemov, Penelope. "Long Life on Death Row." **Governing Magazine**, March 1996: 30.

Linebaugh, Peter. "The Farce of the Death Penalty." **The Nation**, Aug. 14, 1995: 165.

Link, David. "Storyville: Turning Every Issue into a Drama Is Warping Public Policy." **Reason**, Jan. 1995: 35.

Parloff, Roger. "How Determined Lawyers Fought to Save One Man's Life." **Kirkus Reviews**, May 1, 1996.

Pennington, Judy. "Helen Prejean, Nun, Anti-Capital Punishment Author and Activist." **The Progressive**, Jan. 1996: 32.

"Pope Decries 'Culture of Death.'" **The Christian Century**, April 12, 1995: 384.

Robbins, Tim. "On Death Row; Interview with Sister Helen Prejean." **Interview**, Jan. 1996: 40.

Roberts, Steven V. "The Murderer Who Was Too Pathetic to Kill." **U.S. News & World Report**, Aug. 7, 1995: 8.

Rosenberg, Tina. "Death Row's Women Prisoners." **Harper's Bazaar**, Feb. 1996: 110.

Scheer, Robert. "Death Trap; Capital Punishment." **Playboy**, June 1995: 53.

Smolowe, Jill. "Must This Man Die?" **Time**, May 18, 1992: 40.

Stevenson, Bryan. "The Hanging Judges." **The Nation**, Oct. 14, 1996: 16.

Stewart, David O. "The Court Cannot Escape the Issue of Capital Punishment." **American Bar Association Journal**, Nov. 1994.

Stewart, David O. "Defendants Face Barriers in Habeas Challenges to Convictions." **American Bar Association Journal**, April 1993.

Stumbo, Bella. "Executing the Murderer: The Victim's Families Speak Out." **Redbook**, Nov. 1995: 58.

Taylor, Stuart Jr. "Crying Wolf on Death Row." **The American Lawyer**, March 1995: 52.

Taylor, Stuart Jr. "Guilty and Framed." **The American Lawyer**, Dec. 1995: 75

Thomas, Cal. "Death Penalty Helps Protect Innocent Life." **The Montgomery Advertiser**, March 29, 1996.

"US Supreme Court Refuses to Reopen Capital Punishment Cases." **The Progressive**, March 1993: 10.

Valente, Judith. "The Life Penalty; Her Despairing Death Wish Denied." **People**, Feb. 19, 1996: 95.

Van Wormer, Katherine. "Those Who Seek Execution: Capital Punishment as a Form of Suicide." **USA Today**, March 1995: 92.

Varnum, Steve J. "A Barely Tolerable Punishment." **Christianity Today**, Sept. 11, 1995: 19.

Book References

Gatrell, V.A. **The Hanging Tree: Execution & the English People** 1770-1868, 1994, OUP.

It's All the Rage: Crime & Culture, 1995, Addison-Wesley.

Josephson, Barney R. **Humane Reciprocity: The Moral Necessity of the Capital Penalty**, 1979, Ann Arbor Bk.

Kaminer, Wendy. **It's All the Rage**, 1996, Addison-Wesley.

Kempf, Michael J. **America on Death Row**, 1993, From Blues to Bless.

Koosed, Margery B., ed. & intro. **Capital Punishment**, 3 vols., 1996, Garland.

Laurence, John. **The History of Capital Punishment**, 1983, Carol Pub. Group.

Marquart, James W., et al. **The Rope, the Chair, & the Needle: Capital Punishment in Texas**, 1923-1990, 1994, U of Tx Pr.

Martin, Robert P. **The Death Penalty: God's Will or Man's Folly?** 1991, Simpson NJ.

Mello, Michael. **Against the Death Penalty: The Relentless Dissents of Justices Brennan & Marshall**, 1996, NE U Pr.

Miller, Kent S. & Radelet, Michael L. **Executing the Mentally Ill: The Criminal Justice System of the Case of Alvin Ford**, 1993, Sage.

Nakell, Barry & Hardy, Kenneth A. **The Arbitrariness of the Death Penalty**, 1987, Temple U Pr.

Nardo, Don. **Death Penalty**, 1992, Lucent Bks.

Potter, Harry. **Hanging in Judgment: Religion & the Death Penalty in England**, 1993: Continuum.

Prejean, Helen. **Dead Man Walking: An Eyewitness Account of the Death Penalty in the United States**, 1994, Random.

Radelet, Michael L., et al. **In Spite of Innocence: Erroneous Convictions in Capital Cases**, 1992, NE U Pr.

Reed, Emily F. **The Penry Penalty: Capital Punishment & Offenders with Mental Retardation**, 1993, U Pr of Amer.

Rommel, Bart. **Execution: Tools & Techniques**, 1990, Loompanics.

Ryan, Perry T. **The Last Public Execution in America**, 1992, P T Ryan.

Sheleff, Leon S. **Ultimate Penalties: Capital Punishment, Life Imprisonment, Physical Torture**, 1987, Ohio St U Pr.

Siegel, Mark, et al. eds. **Capital Punishment: An Effective Punishment?** 1994, Info Plus TX.

Spear, Charles. **Essays on the Punishment of Death**, 1994, Rothman.

Steins, Richard. **The Death Penalty: Is It Justice?** 1993, TFC Bks NY.

Streib, Victor L., ed. **A Capital Punishment Anthology**, 1993, Anderson Pub Co.

When the State Kills, 1989, Amnesty Intl USA.

White, Welsh S. **The Death Penalty in the Eighties: An Examination of the Modern System of Capital Punishment**, 1987, U of Mich Pr.